Understanding Calvinism

Examining Calvinism's thinking, behavior, and Language

By

Anonymous

This work is published with permission of the author.

ISBN: 9798322550358

TABLE OF CONTENTS

EDITOR NOTES

I was contacted in June of 2017 by a listener going by the name of Duane. He forwarded me a rough copy of this paper and stated it was mine to do with whatever my good discretion would have. I found the paper amazingly engaging and insightful. I had recently started studying the anthropological issues associated with psychology and group behavior. In August of 2016 I had published an episode on "cognitive linguistics". In May of 2017, I published an episode on *Games People Play* on the psychology of human relationships. In November of 2017, I reviewed Scott Adam's book, *Win Bigly*, on convincing people in a post-fact world. In January of 2018, I used Vox Day's book *SJW's Always Lie* to create a podcast showing parallel to Calvinism: Calvinists Always Lie.

I eagerly consume podcasts, YouTube videos, and books related to this subject, so this paper felt like a godsend. It said basically everything I was thinking in a systematic way. When people ask if I wrote this, I always respond with "I wish I did". Although I might have slight disagreements with illustrations or tangential issues, the thrust of the paper was what I was seeking on the issue of Calvinism. My first podcast on this paper was published on July 11, 2017. This was the 80th episode, and the podcast was still only in audio format. Response was lackluster, likely due to format and inaccessibility.

I had always intended to revisit the paper, and an opportunity arose when I finally purchased access to an AI generated voice program. I wanted to test out the features of this software with a short work. This paper seemed like a good fit, but I massively underestimated the size and effort it would take to publish this paper in audio format. Once I began, there was no stopping. It took three months of subscription and 10-20 hours of work to convert the entire work to audio which approximated 4.5 hours. I listened to every word, and had to ensure every concept was audible. Edits were minor, mainly word choice error. The result was lauded by my audience, and they asked for both physical copies and digital.

The timing of this full audio publication came at a beneficial point in the trajectory of the podcast. The audio format was amazingly accessible, and podcast was experiencing peak traffic. This work provides a valuable psychological profile of Calvinism. This is a key concept in the God is Open podcasts, exposing disingenuous actors and explaining how to deal with them. One of my podcast's key contributions to online discourse is exposing how to detect bad faith actors, read their intentions, and disarm them. This work takes a deserved place on the God is Open bookshelf.

Edits have been mainly word choice error and formatting. The sentences are complex and have been left complex. The reader is asked to pardon excessive commas that distinguish complex, embedded thoughts. The text reads as a sophisticated verbal lecture, and the reader is encouraged to take it in such a manner. A few lines were changed for intelligibility.

Understanding Calvinism's thinking, behavior, and Language

Austin Farrer (1904) an Anglican theologian and philosopher, in Faith and Speculation warns that every time man attempts to frame God's providential activity into causal terms, placing God into a chain of sequential causalities, he risks degrading God to the creaturely level, ultimately creating a monstrosity and confusion.

Preliminary note to the Calvinist reader:

If you are a Calvinist reading this, you fall within two possible categories.

(1) Questioning Calvinism: This is understandably the least likely possibility. And in this event, you are in the process of performing your own personal heart-felt inventory, interested in observations of the system from an outsider's point of view. I applaud you, and pray that you continue running the race that is set before you, casting off every weight, being released from any bonds which hold you, ever increasing in making Jesus your first love.

(2) The staunch Calvinist: This is understandably the most likely possibility. And in this event, you are likely in military reconnaissance mode. The follower of Christ does not directly intend to offend others. However, understanding human psychology, one knows that any critique of something, which others are psychologically vested in, will likely result in their experiencing insult or outrage. But, since you are in reconnaissance mode, why not steel yourself as a good soldier and continue on—looking for ways to neutralize the information provided here.

At minimum, the good you may derive from what is presented here is a prospective of the system's sociological characteristics, from an outsider's point of view. As a dedicated Calvinist, you are probably keenly aware that in the realm of marketing "perception rules". So use the information provided here as a means of ascertaining the perception, your potential customer-base has on the product. And as much as possible, please bear in mind, the intent here is not to offend, but to inform.

Introduction:

Many trees of theology have evolved, with naturally occurring controversies ensuing between them. This is probably nowhere more prevalent than with the theology detailed by John Calvin (1509), of France, a trained lawyer and later influential theologian during the 2nd generation of the Protestant Reformation.

Every tree brings forth fruit after its own kind. And the continuation of every species is dependent upon reproduction. One intent for this writing is to help, for a brief moment, lift the fog which obscures the least visible, yet most critical components of Calvinism, with the hopes that once one understands those components, the reason for Calvinist thinking, behavior and language will become evident.

The buyer of precious stones, who does not examine the gem under magnification, is soon parted from his money. This text attempts to help the reader obtain a magnified view of the tree, and its branches. But more importantly, help the reader understand why Calvinists are forced to halt between two opinions, and thus resort to the semantic and argumentation techniques, which predominate their language. When the delineating line between good and evil is breached, and one morphs into the other, making the two almost indistinguishable within the nature and character of God, the expounder is forced to forward his assertions while reflecting benevolence—and confusion is guaranteed.

Part 1. Calvinism's socialization processes—milieu control—a closed system of logic:

The society of Calvinists dramatically differs from mainstream protestant Christianity and Catholicism, in the emphasis it puts on adherence to doctrine. The doctrine becomes a cherished identity marker, and a trophy, which separates the Calvinist from all other Christian groups. The doctrine sets them apart as superior. The doctrine is therefore sacred. Calvinist pastors can be observed brooding over their congregation's assimilation of the doctrine. It is quite common for Calvinist leaders to counsel congregations against exposing themselves to alternative forms of biblical scholarship, no matter how highly that scholarship is recognized internationally. The Calvinist authority structure seeks to exert a much higher degree of control over information. Thus Calvinism sociologically, has for many years, been a closed system, with its own unique values and its own unique language, applying what social psychologists call, milieu control.

The control processes at work within the Calvinist authoritarian social structure controls feedback from group members and refuses to be modified, which results in a closed system of logic. It is consistently observed that Calvinists manifest a pronounced degree of partisanship — an almost obsessive allegiance to the doctrine and to idolized persons, prompting the concern that the respecting of persons within the system is so pervasive, that it may represent a form of seductive entrenchment to which Christian youth are significantly vulnerable.

Over time, the mental conditioning that results goes far beyond simple belief in (or love for) Christ, as Christ is not the central focus of the doctrine. As the individual interacts with others whose minds have become similarly re-formed, the mental conditioning dramatically reinforces itself, and becomes a unique reality which frames all comprehension of things pertaining to God and church.

When the non-Calvinist speaks about God or biblical things, the Calvinist may quite literally hear confusion or heresies, because his mind is so locked into the milieu, and it frames his cognitive perceptions so pervasively, he eventually cannot comprehend any thinking that doesn't affirm it. Free-thinking and personal beliefs are monitored and permitted as long as they do not contradict central dogma.

God-Ungodliness oxymorons are so subliminally assimilated in his concepts of God, that when he speaks, he speaks English. And one thinks they know what he is saying without recognizing when they don't, or understanding how pervasively his frame of reference stems from a good-evil dualistic worldview which the system conditions him to obfuscate, and which eventually becomes his normalcy through the process of internalized acceptance.

These socialization processes are the first step in our ability to understand Calvinistic thinking, behavior, and language.

Part 2: What is truth—notes from Dr. William D. Lutz on DoubleSpeak:

What is reality? Reality is not external. Reality exists not in the mind of the individual, who soon perishes. Reality exists and flourishes from one generation to the next, in the mind of the party; which is collective and immortal. What the party defines as reality - that is real. And how else can the party do that - but by language. The party takes control of language, and takes it away from the individual. And that is where the party gets its power (because those in power who control language control the lens through which people see their world).

Power and doublespeak can be statistically measured and traced in persons within organizations. And the two frequently manifest in proportional measure. Doublespeak is one of the most ancient weapons in social domination games. When the group realizes the manipulative strength of doublespeak, it eventually becomes that group's normalcy. They all speak it to one another quite unconsciously and without even thinking about it. Anyone who achieves power, knowingly or instinctively learns how to use the party's doublespeak with increasing sophistication.

Doublespeak euphemisms, phrases, mantras, and two-faced words become recognized within the group for the powerful tool that they are, for the promotion and defense of the system, and soon everyone in the group who yearns for preeminence becomes its apprentice. And there will always be one who will rise above the rest, prove himself a champion, and become a master in its use, fathering a new generation of doublespeak.

Jesus called his disciples and said: "You see how the Gentiles *Katakyrieu-ousin*, one another—it shall not be so among you." Mark 10:42. Peter warns the shepherds of the flock not to *Katakyrieu-ontes* those in their charge. 1 Peter 4:3. A man controlled by a demon spirit leapt upon them and *Katakyrieu-sas* them. Acts 19:16.

Gaming language is a most potent weapon used by marketers, cunning politicians, lawyers, magicians, and sophisticated groups. Doublespeak then, is a weapon for *Katakyrieu-ousin*. Why did Pilot disparagingly ask Jesus: "what is truth?" Because his was a world of political intrigue, in which men *Katakyrieu-ousin* one another, using both the weaponry of steel and the weaponry of language.

Part 3. Semantic Representations and Power—notes from Steven Pinker The Stuff of Thought:

Within intense and eventful disputes between men, debates are hardly ever about the facts. Most people agree on the facts. Where they differ is in the construal of those facts. How the intricate swirl of matter and space ought to be conceptualized by human minds. And the categories in this dispute, permeate the meanings of words in our language, because they permeate the way we represent reality in our heads.

Semantics is about the relation of words to thoughts. But it is also about the relation of words to reality. It is the way, which parties commit themselves to a shared understanding of truth, and the way their thoughts are anchored to things and situations in the world. It is about the relation of words to a community. Many disputes entail two ways of framing a debate, which are pitted against each other, and the disputants struggle to show that their framing is more apt.

Does stem cell research destroy a ball of cells, or a living human being? Does abortion consist of ending a pregnancy, or of killing a living baby? Does the mainstream Christian find Calvinism distasteful because he is a carnal-minded, semi-pelagian heretic, who chafes at the bit of God's rule, or because glorified-evil, and Calvinist tactics are outside his ethical boundaries? Are Calvinist assertions motivated by a divinely inspired, and righteous desire to glorify God, or a Diotrephes urgency for preeminence, and the need to *Katakyrieu-sas* all who are deemed competitors?

Competing disputes, can be likened to the game: "king of the hill", where power is exercised in the form of semantic representations. The party who can ultimately define and label itself as "holy" and the other as "evil", wins the game and dominates the hill. In this game, words become weapons of destruction - history is rewritten by the victor—and truth is redefined by the conqueror.

Part 4: Recognizing the structure of a house:

The roof of a house does not stand upon a platform of thin-air. Underlying structure must support it. Siding, shutters, doors, windows, and ornate facing all require underlying support. It is critical to be able to differentiate those components, which are ornamental, from those, which are structural. And every house must have a foundation. Many who have sought to examine the house of Calvinism, have done so by concentrating on its ornamental components, without recognizing the foundation upon which those components rest. Many have sought to focus their examination on its acronym TULIP. Such an examination will often produce negative returns, simply because the components under examination are in fact merely ornamental, while the underlying foundational structure upon which the surface components exist, is left undisclosed.

Part 5. The underlying substratum—the foundational proposition:

Calvinism is dedicated to the proposition that God conceives, determinatively causes and meticulously renders certain, all events, which occur in time. For

Calvin, this proposition functions as the underlying substratum and foundation of understanding of every aspect of God's relationship to creation, and Calvin accepts it without question. This proposition is the foundation, cornerstone, and template upon which every additional aspect of the house is built. Since it functions as the underlying foundation for the system, it is also the least visible component. And since it is a philosophical construct, it is the one the Calvinist is least likely to reveal.

Calvin reasons that if a person [P] has a thought [T] at moment [M] which them becomes event [E], then [E] obtained inevitable, and unavoidable, because God conceived, determinatively caused, and then meticulously rendered certain [E] would obtain in such a way as to make [E] compulsatory. And conversely, that God allows no alternative of [E] to ever obtain. For Calvin, God has created a world in which only what God determinatively causes and meticulously controls and renders certain will ever obtain. The causal mechanism through which God accomplishes this, Calvin asserts as divine immutable decrees.

Calvin reasons that in such a world, if person [P] becomes saved, at moment [M], and this then becomes a salvific event [S] for [P], then God wanted [S] for [P] to obtain I such a way that is causally compulsatory. And conversely, if God does not want [S] for [P] to obtain, then [S] for [P] is not possible. In this causally determined world, God gives absolutely no alternative possibilities to the creature. Only what God conceives, determinatively causes, and meticulously renders certain is possible.

On this view, the reason any person is saved or not, has nothing causally to do with the person, nor does it have anything to do with the condition of the person. The reason a person is saved or not is because God designs each person for his or her perspective purpose. Here Calvinists may appeal to Paul's potter and clay analogy, where they resolve, a saved person; one who is designed by God as a vessel of honor vs. a damned person; one who is designed by God as a vessel of wrath.

Calvin further asserts that God establishes totalistic causation for every event, for each individual, millennia before the individual exists in time. In Calvin's words, God determines each mans "LOT" in life, and does so at the foundation of the world.

Calvinist theologian R. C. Sproul enunciates the underlying proposition by asserting: "If there is one single molecule in this universe running around loose, God is not God". And Calvinist Paul Helm asserts: "Not only is every atom and molecule, every [thought and desire], kept in being by God, but every twist and turn of each of these is under the direct [control] of God".

Calvinist Robert R. McLaughlin, in his work: The Doctrine of The Divine Decree states it as: "The Omniscience of God merely programmed into the divine decrees all our thoughts, motives, decisions and actions, which include our sins and failures as well as our successes". Calvin enunciates every faculty of man as causally determined, by stating: "Man by the righteous impulsion of God does that which is unlawful" (Institutes 1-16)

William Lane Craig, an American Christian apologist, philosopher and theologian, identifies the underlying proposition upon which Calvinism is founded as: "Universal Divine Causal Determinism". God solely causally initiates and meticulously controls, every event that obtains—universally, exclusively, immutably, and without any limitation.

Calvinist, Dr. James N. Anderson, of the Reformed Theological Seminary, Charlotte NC, in his published work Calvinism and the first sin, states the underlying proposition: "It should be conceded at the outset, and without embarrassment, that Calvinism is indeed committed to divine determinism: the view that everything is ultimately determined by God.....take it for granted as something on which the vast majority of Calvinists uphold and may be expressed as the following: "For every event [E], God decided that [E] should happen and that decision alone was the ultimate sufficient cause of [E]." Dr. Anderson also states that

Calvinism is committed to a compatibilist form of free will.

Since the underlying proposition is automatically presupposed, it becomes, and most often subconsciously, the single concept which controls every aspect of the Calvinist's perception of God. And because it is presuppositional, it consistently works as an invisible barrier to coherent dialog with non-Calvinists, and a multitude of fruitless disputes perennially occur over controversies, simply because the non-Calvinist doesn't recognize the underlying presupposition, and Calvinists are consistently unlikely to enunciate it. Such dialog is as successful as two ships attempting to exchange cargo, while passing each other in the night. In other words, the two parties spend countless hours speaking past one another. The non-Calvinist walks away perplexed, and the Calvinist walks away feeling misunderstood, and rightly so.

Calvin eventually addresses the question of whether God can "allow" or "permit" events in time to occur. And here Calvin forcibly rejects all such considerations, calling them repulsive (in Calvin's vernacular; "odious" —Concerning the Eternal Predestination of God, p.176). For Calvin, the idea that God merely allows an event to obtain, would seriously compromise God's divine right to directly cause and meticulously control all events through compulsatory causation. Such an idea for Calvin is simply unthinkable, and he would waste no time and direct no small number of harsh pejoratives at anyone who would to any degree, compromise God's sovereignty. With Calvin, often using *Appeal to Divine Rigor* in regard to God, or *Argumentum Ad Hominem*, in regard to detractors, there is no tolerance for any compromise to God's absolute monarchical control over all events.

Calvin's doctrine can be seen as a form of governance known as monarchical absolutism, or simply absolutism, which Calvin has superimposed on God and His cosmos. In monarchical absolutism, a critical attribute of the monarch is "sovereignty", and the doctrine asserts that the monarch cannot be held accountable to any humanly known standard of ethics. In most cases, the "divine right of unaccountability" is said to be endowed upon the monarch by a God.

In the Egyptian dynasty, the monarch was Pharaoh, and the god Horus. Shulgi of Sumeria, (21st century BC) declared himself divine. In Rome, Caesar was declared "Pontifex Maximus", (Bridge builder between heaven and earth), which would be later ascribed to the Roman Pope. This "man-god ruler" model was the predominant form of governance world-wide, throughout the human time-line until about the 19th century.

During Calvin's day, monarchical absolutism appeared in the form of the "The Divine Right Of Kings", where it was asserted as a "doctrine of Grace" and defended by Protestants of the Reformation mostly for political reasons. It is possible Calvin simply saw absolutism as the divine model.

In obsessively adhering to his underlying proposition, Calvin paints himself into a corner, where he is eventually forced to depict through its lens, God's role in evil events. In his voluminous writings, Calvin will make depictions of God's conduct, which will implicitly infer a God who is predisposed towards evil as either heartless aggression in order to display voluntaristic utilitarian prowess or of deriving pleasures from torture. Such conduct from God is defended as his "Divine Right", often with appeals to the words of Paul; "who are you oh-man to reply against God". Calvin's representations of God in this fashion have caused no small measure of discomfort among scripture readers who see scripture consistently representing God's predisposition towards evil as one of reluctance, based upon an over-arching predisposition towards benevolence. But for Calvin, benevolence is irrelevant under the shadow of God's sovereignty, as are ethics, because sovereignty is the supreme attribute and "Divine Right" of the king (i.e., God).

Calvin acquires his unflinching hold on this underlying proposition by his ardent admiration for Augustine (354 – 430 A.D), an early Roman Catholic theologian, philosopher, and bishop of Hippo, in Algeria. Calvinists historically applaud Augustine as the philosophical and theological father of the system.

Part 6. The human psyche and the color of syncretism:

If you've ever been in a store where people buy paint, you've probably seen the mixing of primary colors, very precisely measured into a base color. This mixing process results in a well-controlled final color. We humans find it easy to mix paints together. If, for example, we mixed white with blue, our final color would result in a light blue. Easy, right? But once those two colors are mixed together, it is not easy for us to examine the resulting color and discern the original blue from the original white—its virtually impossible. Nor is it possible for us to separate the white and the blue, back into their original forms.

Now lets say someone mixed various paints into one, and sold it to you claiming it was the original. Firstly, you would find it highly difficult to discern what the original colors were. And secondly, if you placed a high degree of trust in that person, you would be inclined to believe what you were told, which is a reflection of your psyche. Perhaps this is what the scripture means when it says "The word of God is quicker than a two edged sword, dividing soul from spirit". Syncretism works the same way.

When components from various religions are synchronized together, we no longer have the original, but instead we have a final result, based on a mixture, which we embrace as the original. We may be psychologically invested in the assertion that our resulting religion is the superior and pure one. And we may blindly and forcefully assert it as the original, just because we have an emotional need to perceive it as such. Thus the color of syncretism often reflects the color of the human psyche.

Without the Holy Spirit, we don't have the ability to discern what is of the soul and what is of the spirit within ourselves. Nor do we have the ability to divide them. And we can't even start such an investigation if we've been taught to deny it can't possibly happen to us, or to deny a mixture exists, or simply if our psyche depends upon it not existing. That is the color of syncretism. And we currently see numerous theologies, which are thoroughly syncretistic; with each heavily vested in claiming theirs as the original. One observation we sadly recognize among their tactics is to take their unique distinctive syncretistic form of Christianity, and superimpose it on all things honored in the early church, surreptitiously deceiving people into believing the syncretistic system is the original.

Part 7. The human condition—moneychangers—and dependency:

What does a drug dealer do, when he wants to establish a new client? He gives out free samples of the drug. He presents himself as benevolent, coming to the clients aid in time of need. But the underlying methodology is to establish within the client, a relationship of dependency. Slowly, yet gradually, delight inches its way towards addiction within the unsuspecting. As the dependency becomes entrenched, the dealer starts to require various forms of reimbursement. After all, money doesn't grow on trees.

Cable networks may first establish themselves as commercial free. However, once the necessary clientele have become sufficiently invested—in come the commercials, which was the plan from the beginning. Campaigning politicians are prone to make promises, which government moneychangers quietly know cannot possibly be kept. But such promises work wonderfully at drawing in individuals who are inclined to trust. We are, in fact, surrounded by goods and services, which we are quite dependent upon. We go about busy lives from one dependency to another without allowing ourselves to consider the consequences of our dependencies. Dependencies are a reality of our nature—our physical and psychological makeup.

The ancient art of priest-craft operates on and monopolizes the understanding of how easy it is to draw people into psychological dependencies using religion. The priests of Egypt were experts at using religious concepts as a platform from which to exploit the masses. Exploitation produces wealth, privilege, and power.

Every society has its priests and moneychangers, which operate in both secular and religious garb. And the masses will always be taught to see these persons in a benevolent light. Right now a ministry is selling tiny plastic packets of tap water, advertised as holy water, which can cure any financial or physical ailment. These ministries flourish and become the "rich-man" which Jesus compared to a camel going through the eye of a needle. And why is it, when the disciples heard this, they were greatly astonished—because our societies indoctrinate us into perceiving such men in the best light. The very men who are experts, either wittingly or unwittingly, at drawing us into relationships of dependency, we are taught to trust. And once the dependency is established, we are not inclined to escape its ensnarement. Because we have a vested interest in making believe, ensnarement couldn't possibly happen to us, or doesn't exist.

Part 8. Calvin's undying adoration for all things Augustine:

One of the decisive developments in the western philosophical tradition was the eventual widespread merging of the Greek philosophical tradition with the Judeo-Christian religious and scriptural traditions. In the embryonic development of Roman Catholicism, Augustine is one of the main figures through, and by whom this merging was accomplished. Of the Greek philosophical traditions, none influenced Augustine's theology more than Neoplatonism.

Neoplatonism became widely influential at around the 3rd century A.D. and persisted until shortly after the closing of Plato's Academy in Athens at around 520 A.D. After Plato's death (approximately 347 BC), various Greek schools of thought vied to claim the name of Plato for their tradition, with each claiming theirs as the premier representative of Plato's thought. One such school, which rose to predominance, was that of Neoplatonism. Neoplatonism was essentially the works of Plato framed into religious form. The Roman Catholic Church recognized Plato's prowess within the pagan Neoplatonist's religio-philosophy, and Catholicism assimilated Neoplatonism. Neoplatonism represented a great horn of power, and any religion that could claim it as a possession hoped to obtain a place of domination with it.

For nine years prior to Neoplatonism, Augustine was a disciple of a semi-Christian Gnostic dualistic sect known as Manichaeism. Christian Gnosticism asserted a significant presence in its day and the Gnostic sect of Manichaeism flourished in the ancient world. Manichaeism spread with extraordinary speed through both the east and west, from North Africa to China. Being widely promoted by apostles, it reached Egypt at around 240 A.D., and Rome at around 280 A.D. The Roman Emperor Galerius issued the Edict of Toleration in 311 A.D., which ended the Diocletianic persecution of Christianity. Manichaean monasteries existed in Rome in 312 A.D. during the time of the Catholic Pope, Miltiades.

In 312 A.D. Constantine defeated the Roman emperor Maxentius and marched into Rome, bearing his rival's severed head as a trophy, and assumed control. After the usual celebrations and gladiator spectacles, he built the arch of Constantine, displaying himself in the lineage of Roman conquers, depicting the sun god Apollo, along with other Roman gods. Constantine would later present the pope Miltiades with the Lateran Palace, which would become the papal residence and the seat of Catholic governance.

From then on the Roman church grew in political power, and soon carried forward the Roman tradition of domination, occasionally rioting and killing those who posed opposition. Traces of the assimilation of paganism are visible everywhere at Catholic sites. Catholics adoringly touch statues of Pan, Jupiter and the goddess Isis and child, being told they are David, Peter, and Mary with Jesus.

It is an undisputed fact that the lineage of Catholic doctrines evolved in a significantly syncretistic manner. This is a period of time, during which the Roman church was becoming a dominating world power, and in its growth, it consumes and adds to itself, the distinctions of every form of paganism. The syncretistic processes of evolution at this time cannot be understated. And the realization of the tree becoming hybrid is inevitable. Rather than wrestle against principalities and powers, the tradition was to co-op them. History will then evidence the burning to the stake of young mothers for teaching their children the Lords prayer, or families for reading scripture, and the massacre of whole villages.

English historian, Theodore Maynard, in The story of American Catholicism writes: "It has often be charged... that Catholicism has been overlaid with many pagan incrustations. Catholicism is ready to accept that charge - and to make it her boast. The great god Pan is not really dead, he is baptized."

In the Neoplatonist world-view, all things have an infinite, timeless, and unchangeable God as the cause of their existence. Some of the dualistic elements within

Manichaeism were also shared, as Neoplatonism was heavily influential among the Gnostics. For Neoplatonists it would be possible to categorize both "good" and "evil", as "good" or "less good" and possibly not "evil" at all, since all things emanate from the "one", and the "one" is beautiful and good. Therefore, all things exist in the "one", in the form of undifferentiated unity, as elements divinely synchronized within the "one"; of necessity containing good and evil along with all other constituents of the cosmos. Sin and evil can then be stated as beautiful and good, since they are necessary parts of the wholeness of the "one". These constructs would be imbibed by the Catholic Neoplatonists, and Augustine would carry them forward, and in his eloquent writing, baptize them as Christian, just like the great god Pan.

Augustine asserts the good-evil dualism, where he writes: "And because this orderly arrangement maintains the harmony of the universe by this very contrast, it comes about that evil things must need be. In this way, the beauty of all things is in a manner configured, as it were, from antitheses, that is, from opposites: this is pleasing to us even in discourse". (ord 1.7.19)

The subtle nuance in Augustine's synthesis is that it has God requiring evil in order to be whole, or at least for His goodness to be fully actualized and manifested. This concept reappears within modern Calvinist enunciations where it is asserted that God needs to send people to eternal torment (i.e., manifest evil) in order to manifest good. Without the flowery eloquent language, this is simply called "yin-yang".

The worldview of Gnostic good-evil dualism, will then frame Calvinist enunciations of God and cosmos, which manifest in the form of subtle god-ungodliness oxymorons, which the non-Calvinist cannot possibly recognize, because he doesn't understand the underlying worldview which frames them.

One of Neoplatonism's most prominent pagan teachers, Plotinus taught that a person must turn inward to find God, who is identical with the inner reality of the soul. Plotinus was considered a monist, intellectual mystic, and a genius in argumentation. Author, Stephen MacKenna in *The Influence of Plotinus Traced in St. Augustine* observes within Augustine's *Confessions* evidences of at least two mystical meditation experiences, which clearly follow the Neoplatonic model.

Mystic meditation was a practice emphasized by the Neoplatonist's to aid the believer in becoming assimilated into the "one". Plotinus himself however rebuked Gnosticism's good-evil dualism, writing against it in his ninth tractate of the second Enneads which he titled: "Against Those That Affirm The Creator of The Cosmos and The Cosmos Itself to Be Evil".

Neoplatonists held that everything existed only to the extent to which it participated in the "one". For the Christian Neoplatonist, spiritual growth was not marked by the manifestation of good works, but by passively experiencing the "one".

Augustine would carry this forward by formulating that union with God, in knowledge and love, supplants obedience to the Lord, along with any possible reward for faithful service. J. Patout Burns, in *Theological Anthropology* states: "As liberty matures [implying Neoplatonist maturity] the person ceases to deliberate and decide; [implying the loss of independent volition] he gives himself ever more fully and spontaneously, to the increasingly manifest and attractiveness of God."

This enunciation of spiritual growth bears an uncanny resemblance to what is known as gradual entrenchment by a counterfeit force, sighted in cases of possession, in which the individual gradually relinquishes volition or faculties to a counterfeit spirit.

Other elements found in Gnosticism, which will reappear are the doctrine of individual election and the doctrine of the "divine spark", which was the Gnostics way of enunciating that man was totally unable to respond to God's salvific outreach and thus requires a "divine spark" in order to be vivified to salvation.

This then parallels the Calvinist assertion that salvation precedes faith. The Gnostics may enunciate that men are born into different "fields". Some are borne into the "field" of salvation, while others into a "field" of corruption, and therefore utterly lost from birth. We see this concept paralleled within the Calvinist terminology of two "domains of providence" and "total depravity".

Augustine corresponded by letter to a close friend Nebridius, who praises how Augustine's letters: "speak of Christ, Plato and Plotinus". The recognition of intense syncretism here is unavoidable. Catholic Platonists used Platonic concepts as a lens through which they believed they could more clearly see and understand the nature and character of God. Even today, one will find advertisements for Christian academic materials positing this sentiment. The doctrines of Plotinus are advertised as providing a superior understanding of scripture.

Sparks Notes: "Augustine's lasting influence lies largely in his success in combining the Neoplatonic worldview with the Christian one. In Augustine's hybrid system, the idea that all creation is good in as much as it exists, means that all creation, no matter how nasty or ugly, has its existence only in God. Because of this, all creation seeks to return to God, who is the purest and most perfected form of the compromised being enjoyed by individual things. Again, then, any story of an individual's return to God is also a statement about the relationship between God and the created universe:

namely, everything tends back toward God, its constant source and ideal form."

Part 9. Dualistic Cosmology's effect on exegesis vs. the people of the book:

Greek Cosmology represents man's focus on three primary concerns: Origins, Evolution, and Fate, while Greek Teleology represents man's focus on Purpose. As a result, laws of causation were of interest to Greek intellectuals. In Hellenized world, those who lacked analytical knowledge of these things were construed as walking in a form of ignorance.

An intellectual such as Augustine would certainly not want to perceive himself as member of the blind and ignorant masses. Greek intellectualism, applied considerable force into the intellectual world of Augustine's day. This readily explains, Augustine's intellectual venture through the highly popular semi-Christian Gnostic system of Manicheanism and the highly popular pagan system of Neoplatonism.

In contrast to this, the preponderance of Jewish world-view was based upon Hebrew Scriptures, which had been meticulously copied throughout Jewish history. Many Greeks looked disparagingly upon Hebraic concepts as a reflection of primitive, ignorant thinking. The Jewish people had been long classified as the "people of the book".

The pattern we see in Scripture reflects its author's focus. For them, a concern with a Platonic analysis of the cosmos would be as valuable as arguing over how many angels fit on the head of a pin. For the people of the book, such thinking is simply blind speculation and egotistical intellectualism.

There were a few Jewish intellectuals who found Platonic concerns tantalizing. But not so as to dramatically affect the Jewish traditional understanding of God and His relationship to man, and not so as to dramatically affect the Jewish exegesis of scripture. But this is not the case for Augustine.

A cursory review of Manichaeism's doctrinal worldview reveals a system that is deeply affected by Greek, Parthian, Middle Classic Persian, Coptic, Chinese, and Zoroastrian concepts.

Twins are a consistent conception within many pagan religions and cultures around the world. In some, they are seen as ominous and in others as auspicious. Twins in mythology are often cast as two halves of the same whole, sharing a bond deeper than that of ordinary siblings, or otherwise shown as fierce rivals. The concept of twins also appears within some religions as a dualistic cosmos.

The gods Apollo and Artemis are twins. The god Pan appeared in either a benevolent, or malevolent form. In

Hinduism, the Ashwini Twins or Ashvins are the Healers who are also offered sacrificial offerings or oblations as per the Rig Veda. In Xingu mythology of Brazil, the twin brothers Kuat and Iae forced the evil king Urubutsin to give light to the world, and Kuat became the sun with Iae as the moon. The Egyptian creation story included the earth god Geb and the sky goddess Nut, who were twins.

As we start to approach the cultures and times that would have more influenced Augustine, we have Basilides, (117 AD), who taught a form of Gnosticism, which incorporated the dualistic deity Abraxas, and he claimed to have inherited his teachings from Matthew.

But the dualistic system that would have been of greatest influence, would be the Zoroastrian system, incorporated into Manichaeism, having twin gods Ahriman and Ahura Mazda, who represent divine-evil and divine-good. Manichaeism therefore taught that the cosmos contains an opposition of two principles, good and evil, each equal in relative power and necessity. And thus we have a dualistic cosmos in which good and evil share equal divine status.

When a dualistic cosmology and a Neoplatonic view of God are synchronized with the monotheistic God of Christianity, what will appear is an immutable God whose relationship to good and evil are utilitarian. Scriptures, which speak of God repenting of making man, or giving man the choice between life and death, become a curiosity, because the Neoplatonic God is immutable, (i.e., unchangeable) and therefore cannot change his mind or give choices to his creatures.

Such scriptures must be allegorized or interpreted with complex non-explicit distinctions in order to be rightly understood. Scriptures in the New Testament that speak of predestination can readily be interpreted in the framework of the Gnostic good-evil dualism, where those individuals who are predestined to the light are awakened by the divine spark, while others are destined to the dark.

Both acts of predestination are equally holy, because both manifest the glory of the "one". The believer would learn how to compartmentalize a good-evil dualism, stoicism, and to love and desire a utilitarian god.

The Manicheans are definitely not "people of the book". As such, their focus reached out much farther than the simple worldview found within the authors of scripture. Gnostic urgencies therefore do not fit the biblical pattern of being simply focused on man's right relationship to his creator.

Manichaeistic thinking was a labyrinth of complex, multi-layered, and highly detailed explanations, concerning the origins and evolution of divine beings and man. Augustine will become its intellectual disciple for nine years of his life, and fully embrace many of its concepts. For him, to transition out of its complex labyrinth on his intellectual journey towards Catholicism is going to take years of intellectual, analytical contemplation.

Augustine is not one to simply throw away concepts that he has previously embraced as infallible truth. He is persuadable, but as he grows older and his power and influence increase within the Catholic monarchical system, his evolving theology becomes reliant upon his own internal critical faculties. Manichaestic and Neoplatonic concepts deemed honorable must be tweaked in order to fit, and emerge as a Catholic neo-orthodox theology.

Because of these influences, Augustine's thinking does not fit the biblical pattern of being focused simply on man's relationship to God. Augustine's need to avoid being a member of the blind and intellectually ignorant masses, so looked down upon by Greek intellectualism, forces him to go beyond the biblical focus, and therefore beyond the biblical pattern.

Additionally, the post apostolic fathers never had such intense Platonic influences born upon them, and Augustine thus cannot rely upon them as legitimate sources, compared to the sophisticated Platonic thinking of his day. Therefore, the urgencies, which drive Manichaeistic thought, and the urgencies which drive Neoplatonic thought, become urgencies which influence Augustine's exegesis. Thus, Augustine's insatiable intellectual quest impels him to journey to places where no high-standing Christian theologian has ever gone before.

It's ironic, how syncretism contributes to raising Augustine, to be lauded as one of the great-ones in his theological tradition. It has often been said that arrogance is the dark side of knowledge. One of the fruits of the Augustinian tradition will be its reputation for exhibiting a self-applauding air of superiority within the Calvinist fold.

The Augustinian tradition therefore inherently lends itself to things Jesus pointed out as disdainful. Such as straining at exegetical gnats while swallowing the camels of Manichaeism and Neoplatonism. An insistence upon the best seat in the synagogue of Christian theologies. To be lauded as great ones in the Christian marketplace. A proud repetitive exhibition of wide stoic phylacteries. A love for being honored by men, and making sure the outside of the cup appears clean, when the inside is full of linguistic magicianry.

At around 418 A.D. Augustine produced two treaties, "On the grace of Christ" and "On original sin". Many did not hesitate to agree with Augustine's assertion that the salvation process is totally dependent upon unmerited favor. But they were in no way comfortable with Augustine's insistence that God did not allow an individual the freedom to dissent—sighting it as a form of inescapable ensnarement. It does bear an uncanny resemblance to a mystical potion or spell—a type of seduction, or divine-magic. It could be seen as a mode of human inducement common within the occult, and therefore antithetical and abhorrent to a (Holy) Spirit.

They additionally disagreed with Augustine's assertion that no amount of sinning could affect ones salvation. Augustine responded to these objections, and disputes over these issues would continue perennially—now known as Augustine's controversial doctrines of predestination, which Calvin would later adoringly carry forward.

The scripture says that all see through a glass darkly. The question then remains, which glass. For Augustine, that lens was a combination of Gnosticism, Christ, Plato, and Plotinus. For Calvin, Augustine became the only right lens through which one views scripture. And the tree continues to bring forth fruit after its kind.

Part 10. Questions—The "why" and "how" concerning events which come to pass:

With Universal Divine Causal Determinism functioning as the center of his universe, Calvin's answers are fairly consistent. For the question of "why" events come to pass—the answer is most often "for God's good pleasure".

For the question of "how" events come to pass—the answer is most often "all events are ordained at the foundation of the world by immutable decrees". Where this becomes most problematic, is when these answers are automatically applied to the "why" and "how" of evil events which come to pass.

Calvin writes: "Nor ought it to seem absurd when I say, that God not only foresaw the fall of the first man, and in him the ruin of his posterity; but also at his own pleasure arranged it" (Institutes 3 23 7).

There are hideously evil events, which come to pass. For example, a young child is raped, her body cut into peace's and buried. Or an event where employees of a chicken-nugget processing factory were murdered and their bodies discovered in the breaded nugget product, distributed to various restaurants.

Such events are terribly hideous, and yet they fall into Calvin's universal category of all things that "come to pass". And thus Calvinism's answer to the "why" and "how" applies universally. So of course this begs the question: Does the Calvinist construe, that God ordains such events for his good pleasure?

If one is to remain rationally consistent to Calvin's universal assertions, it most certainly must be a forgone conclusion; else man threatens to compromise God's good pleasure or His sovereignty. We should then readily understand "why" and "how" Calvinists navigate around these topics, and fiercely reject any rational conclusions that threaten the radiant luster of the sacred object to which they are significantly invested.

If the Calvinist speaks clearly and unambiguously, he must assert that evil events occur in order to service God's good pleasure, and manifest His sovereignty. However, such a concept would surely fit the model of sadism, which is defined as a deliberate cruelty, and the tendency to derive pleasure, from inflicting pain, suffering or torment upon others.

This puts the Calvinist in an obviously troublesome position, as he is required to assert Calvin's basic propositions for the "why" and "how" of all events. All the rational individual need do is follow Calvin's answer to its logical conclusion in order to recognize, God's conduct is viewed as fitting the model of sadism. And so we can see how taking his reasoning to its logical conclusion backfires on the Calvinist's claim that the system he cherishes is superior, in the light of divine holiness.

Voltaire, (1694), French Enlightenment writer, historian, and philosopher, in The Age of Louis XIV, writes: "It is dangerous to be right in matters on which the established authorities are wrong."

And Jesus went into a synagogue on the Sabbath day, where there was a man with a withered hand. And the Pharisees whose doctrine was bible-based, challenged Jesus asking him if it were God's will to heal on the Sabbath day? — Matthew 12: 1 2. But the man's parents spoke these words to the Pharisees out of fear, because they knew, anyone who confessed Jesus was the Christ would be labeled heretical, and cast out of the synagogue — John 9:22.

Because Calvinist socialization processes include milieu control, there is an emphasis on group conformity and unanimity, such that anything which questions or threatens to cast dispersions on the doctrine is met with negative reinforcements, which may include public humiliation, or punitive correction.

The Calvinist who does not purport himself carefully, can be cast out of the synagogue. Being labeled a "pelagian", for example can represent rejection and demonizing of an individual within the group, since it is frequently used as an extreme pejorative, with demonic connotations. A need for peer acceptance or a subconscious need for family cohesion, may exist within each member, as his individual identity is re-mapped into the group's identity.

As a result of carrot/stick methodology, Calvinists become strongly compelled to honor the sacred object, and to protect it from disparagement, with a militant vigilance reminiscent of the "Brown Shirts" of 1940's Germany.

These socialization processes help explain the behaviors people observe when Calvinists are faced with questions about the system's logical conclusions of glorified-evil. In order to protect the sacred object from criticism, Calvinists exhibit a variety of avoidance strategies.

(1) Using equivocal language to call evil good.

(2) Casting Ad Hominems on the questioner, with accusations of maliciousness towards Calvinism or God.

(3) Categorical denials and refusals to recognize rational conclusions.

(4) Language designed to camouflage the specter of glorified-evil.

(5) Appeal to the "you don't understand us" argument.

(6) Appeal to the inscrutable argument.

(7) Deviating from Calvin's strict "why" and "how" assertions, manufacturing a softer mask over the system, and making it more palatable (i.e., mainstream) by obfuscating its glorified-evil components.

The most Christ-like way of interacting with Calvinists using these tactics, is to understand the demands the system requires of them, as well as the psychological dependencies engendered in them, and treat them with respect and compassion.

But it is also critical; one realizes the degree to which these influences result in their unflinching allegiance, stoicism, ethical compromises, and a language thoroughly permeated with subtleties.

Calvinists are often driven by internally conflicting urgencies.

> (1) The urgency to retain strict allegiance for group peer acceptance or recognition.

> (2) The urgency for recruitment and the expansion of their population.

> (3) The urgency to advertise their system in the most grandiose terms.

> (4) The urgency to stave off or minimize the stigmas of glorified-evil, and godly-evil.

These then become the urgencies that drive Calvinists. And we should quite easily see, how these urgencies drive them to deploy language techniques that are disingenuous. We after all, are still members of a lost and fallen world.

We all sin and fall short of the glory of God. Dishonest language techniques are, in fact, an integral part of what it means to be human. None of us are immune. Every time we step into a grocery store, we are surrounded by dishonest language.

Every time we turn on a TV, we are exposed to dishonest language techniques. We are exposed to these techniques daily, on multiple levels, and in every aspect of our social interactions.

And Calvinism's urgencies have simply driven them to assimilate doublethink, and evolve and perfect their own unique doublespeak language.

Part 11. Calvinism's Four Communication Modes— alternating semantic models:

There is a now-godly-good, now-godly-evil, alternating emphasis, consistent within Calvinistic language. And a recognizable characteristic is the framing of (concept pairs) reflecting a dualistic cosmos. We can also observe linguistic processes, which alternate between four different modes of communication.

(1) THEOLOGICAL-BOASTING mode: Here he is eulogizing God's good pleasure, and God's sovereignty, which entails both glorified-good and glorified-evil. Or he might be lauding the system's image or persons.

(2) THEOLOGICAL-DEFENSE mode: Here he is defending the system's representations of glorified-evil

as necessary, and right. Dualism and Universal Divine Causal Determinism are what make the system superior for him, what gives the system its distinctiveness, and function as phylacteries for him.

But the glorified-evil component is morally problematic. To compensate its impact, the Calvinist will switch to:

(3) AS-IF mode: This is his inventive mode, and his language is often cosmetic in nature. In this mode he might create philosophical inventions AS-IF they were biblical, or represent his own unique understanding of Calvinism, AS-IF it were "core" Calvinism. Or he might communicate AS-IF the systems divine-evil component doesn't exist.

Or he might frame God's causal role in a given event AS-IF it were "active", and then alternate to framing it AS-IF it were "passive". Or man's causal role in a given event AS-IF libertarian free will doesn't exist, and then alternate to framing it AS-IF it does. Or he might frame dualistic sentences, containing mutually exclusive presuppositions, AS-IF their contradiction doesn't exist.

In AS-IF mode, assertions are made solely based on the expediency of the moment, and enunciated AS-IF it they are fully logically coherent. AS-IF mode is quite powerful because recipients may be ill prepared to manage an inexhaustible volume of ad hoc inventions, and semantic subtleties.

(4) PASTORAL mode: Here he utilizes soft-spoken—emotive, religious, or sophistic language to hide the system's glorified-evil components while projecting benevolence. In Pastoral mode, his language is often designed to mimic the language of mainstream Christianity, which, ironically he sternly condemns as soon as he switches back into Theological-boasting mode.

And this tactic of alternating between Theological-boasting mode and Pastoral mode, may be likened to a double-agent, operating within two countries in conflict with each other.

Part 12. Sovereignty becomes God's identity marker:

With causal determinism as the underlying structure of the theology, it's no wonder that Calvinists raise God's sovereignty as the supreme attribute, and Calvinists frequently enunciate sovereignty as the key identifier of God. All other attributes of God may then be implicitly seen as functionally subservient to sovereignty.

For example, a popular Calvinist pastor, John Piper asks the question: "How does a sovereign God exercise his love?" Here the wording clearly infers a hierarchy concerning the attributes of God, where the exercise of God's love is enunciated as subservient to sovereignty.

Calvinist Jonathon Edwards states it as: "The sovereignty of God is his absolute, independent right of disposing of all creatures according to his own pleasure".

Calvinist A.W. Pink states it as: "Can we be too extreme in insisting upon the absoluteness and universality of the sovereignty of God?" And again Pink states: "When we say that God is sovereign in the exercise of his love, we mean that He loves whom He chooses. God does not love everybody."

Sovereignty has been described as the essence of God, the essence of the Gospel, the essence of faith, the essence of Holiness, the essence of love, the essence of wrath, and the essence of Grace.

It is not unrealistic to consider that sovereignty within Calvin's system expands to consume all else. And how easy it is to understand how that would be the case, when one recognizes the underlying foundational construct and lens through which one looks at all of the data of life, is Universal Divine Causal Determinism.Every Calvinist who would ever be lauded as a great Calvinist, has been applauded within the society by his own way of eulogizing God's sovereignty.

It is interesting to note statistically, however, the consistency with which all such enunciations fall short of lifting the curtain so that the foundation (universal divine causal determinism) can be recognized for the indispensable role it plays in producing the "Radical Distinction" that makes Calvinistic sovereignty superior to alternative conceptions, for the Calvinist.

It would not be uncommon to hear a Calvinist accuse alternative theologies as being based upon philosophy or worldliness, and Calvinism based 100% upon scripture. Knowing what we know about the evolution of Christian theology and the role of syncretism within its evolution, what is the statistical probability that such an assertion can ever possibly be believed?

The unfortunate byproduct of what appears to be pervasive system-glorification, is that the vast majority of Calvinists, who trust their perspective author, scholar, pastor, or teacher, when they are told the system consists of the 100% pure solid gold of scripture, happily accept all such eulogistic boasting without the slightest twinge or question, and as naturally as a fish swallows a worm.

The Calvinist is aware that sovereignty that is distinctively Calvinistic will be unpalatable to outsiders. As such he will be careful to confine strict Calvinistic sovereignty to the fold i.e., to insiders who honor them. Whereas in public forums, and published books, his enunciations predominate definitions of sovereignty common to mainstream Christianity, enunciated in Calvinistic terminology, producing the appearance of being distinctives of Calvinism.

But he cannot remain in that mode forever, because enunciating a mainstream definition of sovereignty doesn't support the assertion that Calvinism's distinctive sovereignty is superior. And to that end, straw man definitions of sovereignty can be crafted, easily viewed as aberrant, in order to assert a need for a superior Calvinistic perspective.

David Bentley Hart, an Eastern Orthodox theologian and philosopher writes: "The curious absurdity of all such doctrines is that, out of a pious anxiety to defend God's transcendence against any scintilla of genuine creaturely freedom, they threaten effectively to collapse that transcendence into absolute identity—with the world and the devil. For, unless the world is truly set apart from God and possesses a dependent but real liberty of its own analogous to the freedom of God, everything is merely a fragment of divine volition, and God is simply the totality of all that is and all that happens; there is no creation, but only an oddly pantheistic expression of God's unadulterated power."

Part 13. Viewing God's intentions through the lens of Universal Divine Causal Determinism:

As has been originally stated, Calvin asserts that God's determinative causal-will is effectual for all events universally, and that every event is determined in advance, at the foundation of the world, and prior to the time in which each event will obtain. This over-arching view controls Calvin's perception of God's interactions with humanity described within scripture. For example, Calvin writes concerning the Genesis narrative where God commanded Adam and Eve not to eat of the forbidden tree. Here Calvin notes that Adam and Eve's obedience was not what obtained. Instead, their disobedience obtained— A Posteriori knowledge.

Calvin following his line of reasoning asserts that God must have actually willed Adam and Eve's disobedience or else it would not have been possible to obtain. But this brings into question God's deliberate choice to communicate to Adam and Eve that which was contrary to his real will. Calvin asserts that God must withhold information from his people when he communicates.

Here Calvin creates an Ad Hoc Rescue, claiming that God spoke to Adam and Eve a "Revealed" will. And that God must have withheld from Adam and Eve his true will, which Calvin then construes as God's "Secret" will. Unfortunately, Calvin doesn't address the critical difference between withholding information from someone, and purposefully misleading someone. For Calvin, it logically follows that the only way man can know God's real or "Secret" will, is after a given event obtains— A Posteriori knowledge. As a result, God may represent himself to his people in a way that is in total opposition to His real intentions.

In short, God communicated to Adam and Eve in such a way as to deliberately mislead them about his true intentions for them, leading them to believe what He intended for them was their success in obedience, while simultaneously applying an overwhelming supernatural causal force sufficient to ensure they would not.

A Calvinist argument to support this reasoning could be: "If God truly intended for Adam and Eve to obey, then they would obey, for it is not possible for an event to obtain that is in opposition to what God determines through his immutable decrees. Therefore, it could not be not possible for Adam and Eve to obey, when God's "Secret" will was that they disobey".

And Calvin further reasons that the way we know what God's true will (was, is, or will be), is by simply observing which events obtain— A Posteriori knowledge. In this case Adam and Eve disobeyed. So, Calvin reasons, God's true will was for them to disobey, even though what he communicated to them was the opposite.

Part 14. He loves me—He loves me not—compartmentalized doublethink:

Additional consequences of this line of reasoning become apparent; that God purposefully communicates to his people, and does so strategically with the intent of misleading them about his true intentions.

It then follows that within this view, God applies distinctions, which He does not reveal to His people when He speaks. And this of course raises further questions concerning scripture as it relates to us today, as scripture is held as God's foremost way of communicating to us.

Since we hold that scripture is the breathed word of God, if we then hold, as Calvin does, that God purposefully misrepresents himself when He communicates to His people, how are we to know if what God has communicated within scripture is His "Revealed" will, or his "Secret" will as it concerns us? How do we know if what we read within scripture is applicable to us or not?

Historically, Calvinists have answered this question using words that enunciate distinctions such as God's "prescribed" will vs. God's "decreed" will. In this case, God's "prescribed" will is what we read in scripture, but again God's "prescribed" will is to be distinguished from God's "decreed", "secret", "real" will.

And in a dualistic cosmos, these two wills can be diametrically opposed, which Calvin additionally affirms by stating: "sometimes God causes those whom he illumines only for a time, to partake of it, and then he justly forsakes them on account of their ungratefulness and strikes them with even greater blindness".

The implications are all too clear; that God firstly, determinatively and meticulously leads a person to believe they are elected, saved and bound for heaven. And then at some later point in time determinatively and meticulously renders certain they spend eternity in a lake of fire. Here we have a person, made a believer by God, resting upon pastoral assurances that he can trust what he reads in scripture, with at least a subconscious awareness that God may actually be misleading him. It is no wonder that this would engender a form of doublethink; a cognitive condition in which the believer simultaneously embraces two mutually contradicting beliefs as both true, and the mind learns to compartmentalize these in such a way as to avoid cognitive dissonance.

Father Wilbur Ellsworth, in Journey out of Reformed Theology, states: "There was a young man in the church who came to me. Good, lovely guy. Seriously involved with a young lady, to marry her. I just loved that couple. He came to me one day and said; I am deeply depressed. My soul is dark.

I said; Why?

He said; I don't love God the way I should.

I said; tell me why, what's happening?

He said; I don't love God, as I should because I'm not sure he loves me as much as I need. I'm not sure I'm Elect.

Well if I needed another stab in the heart—that did it. We sat there for 3 hours. Finally, I said to him, if you believe you can't be sure of God's love for you, then I will admit you can't love him as you need to. What does 1st John say? We love because He first loved us. I think this is the cruelest moment I've ever had in my entire ministry. I said to him, If that is your theology, I have nothing to offer you.

He just stared at me. I said, I don't believe for a moment that that is the testimony of scripture. That is not the testimony of the Holy Tradition, of the Church. But if you embrace that theology, I sorrowfully agree with you—you are stuck. We talked for about another 10 minutes, and he left under that weight."

To minimize the degree of consternation this doctrine has had on sincere Calvinists who seek to understand their relationship to God, and to understand God's intentions for them as individuals, some Calvinist pastors have historically taught their congregations, they are to automatically assume God's intentions for them are honorable and retain that as their foremost consideration of God's will.

But one can't help bear in mind that God's real intent for them may be a lake of fire, since that follows from the arguments of Calvin himself. But it is more critical to recognize that in the system; "honorable" as it relates to God, has no *A Posteriori* meaning, because it is not given to the creature to judge what "honorable" means (in relation to God).

The believer is to approach God AS-IF His "Secret" will is their eternal blessing, without really knowing what the *A Posteriori* meaning of "eternal blessing" will be. They will only know what God's "Secret" will be for them at the moment they either arrive in heaven or the lake of torment and fire. At that time they will have *A Posterior* knowledge of what (type) of eternal blessing (heaven or hell), God's good pleasure and immutable decree determined for them.

Some Calvinist pastors have resolved that there is simply no sense in worrying about whether God's intentions for you are heaven or an eternal lake of fire. Calvinist pastor, John Piper states this by asserting that you are to declare, that whatever God does, He will always do "Right".

But again, it logically follows that at this time, it is not given for you to have *A Posteriori* knowledge of what "Right" means. "Right", is whatever God's good pleasure is at any moment, and it is only given for the creature to know what God's good pleasure will be, after it obtains. In this context, the meaning of "Right" becomes arbitrary. In a good-evil, dualistic cosmos,

"Right" could mean good—or it could just as easily mean evil. And this introduces ambiguity into the meanings of words such as "right", "honorable", "righteous" etc. Mainstream Christians readily observe within the teachings of Jesus, how He always maintains a sharp line of demarcation between the concepts of good and evil.

And Jesus never introduces ambiguity to this line of demarcation when referencing the conduct of God. Jesus never depicts God as predisposed to conduct that could be misconstrued as evil, in the ways that Calvin is forced to do. And so the system's consistent blurring of Jesus' line of demarcation between good and evil, has quite naturally been a perennial concern for mainstream Christians.

Calvinists often assert, this element of the system makes it a "superior" understanding of God. James White, an apologist for Calvinism, affirms this sentiment by calling it a more "fully orbed", or more "nuanced" theology. While the mainstream Christian is concerned with its perception of God's relationship to evil as ambiguous, or worse, dishonoring Jesus for the sake of a "superior" theology.

Additionally, Christians readily observe this blurring effect as ubiquitous within all pagan religions. In the occult they see "white and black" witches, and Lucifer is both the "angel of light" and "prince of darkness". In the system of "yin-yang", light and darkness are both fully justified, as they are both necessary components of the "one". Harry Potter uses the same energy that the villain uses, except he uses it for good, while the villain uses it for evil. Does this make Harry Potter a reflection of God? Does Harry Potter's ability to use demonic energy for good, provide a more "fully orbed" way of perceiving God and his cosmos?

David Bentley Hart writes: "For, after all, if it is from Christ that we are to learn how God relates Himself to sin, suffering, evil, and death, it would seem that He provides us little evidence of anything other than a regal, relentless, and miraculous enmity (against sin and death). Sin Jesus forgives, suffering Jesus heals, evil Jesus casts out, and death Jesus conquers. And absolutely nowhere does Christ act as if any of these things are part of the eternal work or purposes of God."

The Old Testament contains a narrative of King Solomon receiving Holy Spirit inspired wisdom from God. And the narrative provides a description of what that wisdom looked like, in the story of two women arguing over their right of ownership to a newborn child.

Solomon tests the (type) of love each woman has for the child by commanding the child be chopped in half. A question might be asked: is Solomon using this strategy as a means of discerning which woman is the biological mother? Or is it possible, Solomon is using it as a means of discerning which woman more reflects the nature and character of God and his intentions for the child? Since Solomon's wisdom is Holy Spirit inspired, the latter would seem plausible. Does God really care about which woman is the biological mother? Or is God's intention that the child would have a mother that loves the child in a way that more reflects His love for mankind?

As the story unfolds, one woman agrees to have the child cut in half, while the other throws herself over the child in a self-sacrificial manner. The Calvinist might be asked, which woman more reflects the nature and character of God? The one who sacrifices her own right of sovereignty over the child, so that the child may live, or the one who would cut the child in half for her good pleasure? If the Calvinist be consistent with Calvin himself, he could easily answer the later.

But we can see how this would put the Calvinist in a difficult position, attempting to remain consistent with Calvin's concept of utilitarian sovereignty. Some would unabashedly say the woman who wanted the child cut in half, more accurately reflects a sovereign, all powerful God who rules the universe solely for his good pleasure.

Others, not so intent on asserting sovereignty would find a way to refute the question, perhaps by asserting they hold God's intentions as only benevolent. But that assertion contradicts Calvin's basic premise that God acts only according to His good pleasure, and the secret council of his will, from which evil cannot be withheld, and which man is not given to know.

In any case, mainstream Christians quite naturally associate the blurring of Jesus' line of demarcation between good and evil, which they observe within Calvin's system, as perhaps a sign of, or indicative of a pagan doctrine.

And one, which dangerously distorts the creature's perception of a God of Holiness and Perfection. The same distorted perception of God that the serpent in the garden introduced to Adam and Eve. In mainstream Christianity the words "holiness", "perfection", and "love" do not have ambiguous *A Posteriori* meanings, because they are aspects of God's character, and His character is determinative of His conduct.

Unlike the doctrine of the "Divine Right of Kings", the mainstream Christian holds that God does subject Himself to His own declared standards of ethics. And Jesus' declarations: "On earth as it is in heaven" and "Be ye Holy as your heavenly Father is Holy" do not have any additional exegetical distinctions imposed on them. Since the mainstream Christian views God's holiness expressed within His moral laws as determinative to His conduct as well as man's, this resolves to one golden standard of morality and ethics, applicable; on earth as it is in heaven. Additionally, the mainstream Christian interprets Jesus' statement: "when you see me, you see the Father", as inferring man's knowledge of God and His conduct, by virtue of *A Posteriori* knowledge of Jesus.

But for Calvin, God's standard of conduct remains shrouded behind a veil, which he calls: "the secret and inscrutable counsel of God". And since this is the case, it is not given for man to have *A Posteriori* knowledge of what "holiness" or "love" means, (as they pertain to God) —which for the mainstream Christian, resolves to a blurring of Jesus' line of demarcation between good and evil.

The mainstream Christian looks aghast at how completely the Calvinist embraces a purely utilitarian God because it is not the God they see reflected in Jesus. And the Calvinist looks at the mainstream Christian who doesn't embrace his utilitarian God and sees a rebellious semi-heretic.

As to whether the Calvinist views Jesus as purely utilitarian, is unknown, as they seem to be strangely quiet about their concepts of Jesus and his character. Because of the Calvinist's negligible emphasis on Jesus, mainstream Christians often comment that Calvinism appears non-Christ-centric. And that seems to make sense, since God and His sovereignty are the system's crown jewels.

Part 15. Double standard leads to doublethink, leads to doublespeak:

The Calvinistic system then resolves to two standards of ethics—one for God which is inscrutable, and one for man, which is expressed by God's moral laws. When the Calvinist is communicating in AS-IF mode, he may appeal to a "Universal Moral Law", As-If it exists in his system. But this assertion is incoherent, because it would logically entail that God adhered to a universal standard. We must remember that in the Calvinist system, only God's sovereignty is universal—all else is limited.

For Calvin, God's morality lies hidden behind a veil, Calvin calls: "the secret counsel of His will". There is however an earthly morality, based upon God's commandments. But that standard of morality is relative only to the creature, and God cannot be held accountable to it, for to do so would compromise His sovereignty. The Calvinist may try to talk his way around this point, but in such case, one would want to be on the lookout for ambiguous word play or self-contradictions.

In response to the "He loves me, He loves me not" syndrome, Calvinist pastors may teach their congregations to simply refuse to believe the least desirable outcome. But it's easy to see how this becomes doublethink, which eventually becomes doublespeak. And outsiders express perennial frustration at trying to understand the doctrine as it is enunciated with doublespeak as a natural part of the language. Outsiders in most cases simply don't know enough about the subtle nuances of the doctrine in order to realize the degree to which doublethink is required, and has been successfully assimilated.

Over numerous generations, Calvinists have developed their own lexicon of terms used to reinforce Calvinist distinctions. God's "prescribed" will is for your salvation, but God's "decreed" will may be for your eternal torment.

And so: "He loves me – He loves me not" quite naturally results in a form of doublethink.

A doublethink version of the good shepherd:

There once was a good shepherd who had 100 totally depraved sheep. For one of the totally depraved sheep, the good shepherd dedicated a room in his house, ensuring it all the lush comforts his good house could provide. The other 99 totally depraved sheep, he sent to a torture chamber to be tortured to death. Once the shepherd's good pleasure was accomplished, he turned to the one totally depraved sheep he had saved and said: "I have saved the one totally depraved sheep and passed over the 99, because the 99 were totally depraved."

Part 16. Unfalsifiable beliefs, ingenious pied pipers, inscrutabilities and endorphins:

Many beliefs are inherently unfalsifiable. Not able to be proven false, but not necessarily true. Such beliefs engender significant numbers of adherents when men of greatness and genius can make them appealing. And they have the added benefit of never being successfully refuted.

Studies have been done within Social Psychology on the observable characteristics of unfalsifiable belief systems. One study was submitted by Justin Friesen, Troy Campbell, and Aaron Kay, to the Journal of Personality and Social Psychology, sighting reasons unfalsifiable belief systems are so appealing.

Certain personality types are drawn to an unfalsifiable belief system because the system requires a high degree of philosophical maintenance, which the psychologists described as both "offensive" and "defensive". Obviously, people who have a bent towards intellectualism are part of the demographics. This demand for philosophical maintenance provides a rich environment for persons of intellectual genius or verbal eloquence to gain notoriety.

Such persons can engineer and maintain highly sophisticated arguments in promotion or defense of the system, which appear wonderfully compelling, and completely rational, but when examined under expert scrutiny, surface logical puzzlements, and are inherently reliant upon sophisticated linguistic maneuvers.

Defending the system can be likened to a chess-game, or sword-fighting with maneuvers which include: attacks, counter-attacks, lunges, thrusts, and going for the jugular; within linguistic disputations—all of which can be highly endorphin producing for the right kind of persona. Another aspect of an unfalsifiable belief system is how readily it can function as a cosmetic mask, which enriches the persona of its adherent.

Gnosticism has been consistently noted as having this quality. Writer Philip J. Lee, in his book; Against the Protestant Gnostics has a chapter devoted to the phenomena of Gnostic elitism where he observes how Gnosticism appeared as a "private" form of Christianity, which he writes: "of necessity correlates to religious elitism". When the self effectively becomes a member of the "elect" or "select" group, set apart from those who are "common" or somehow "unworthy", it quite naturally evolves a persona that subconsciously distinguishes itself and its adherents as superior in some way.

Philip writes: "There is little doubt that Calvin, among other reformers, was strongly inclined towards Augustinian elitism in his suspicion that the great majority of humanity would suffer damnation".

Calvin did warn against spiritual pride, Philip relates. However, such warnings against, and denials of elitism, may only prove to serve as ingenious cosmetics, crafted upon a religious mask, behind which the elitist persona can hide itself from the stigma of spiritual pride.

Philip writes: "With such a determined view of the fate of the damned, it is difficult to see how followers of Calvin could be other than elitist. New England Calvinists, almost from the beginning, saw themselves a spiritual aristocracy."

Cotton Mather, a member of the New England Calvinists for example, insisted that Jesus' intercession only reaches the "elect" of God.

Philip writes: "The glimpse of the 'Pleroma', (divine dualistic powers) so important to the ancient Gnostics, was also the decisive factor in New England Calvinism."

Alvin Plantinga, American analytic philosopher, refers to the appeal of unfalsifiable beliefs when he relates how intellectuals are drawn towards solipsism. A solipsist believes that he is the only real person alive on earth, and all other persons are figments of his imagination. Plantinga muses on the genius of the human mind, which is so capable at compartmentalizing data; relegating data which can be used to affirm the belief as wonderful and legitimate, while scorning data which contradicts the belief, as disdainful and illegitimate.

Imagine you are a solipsist riding in a taxi at high speed down a highway. You believe the cars are real, you are real, and the speed you are traveling is real, but the person driving the car in the front seat is a figment of your imagination. Imagine all of the highly complex and fascinating neurological processes your brain has to accomplish in order to survive and thrive, while tenaciously holding the belief. Thus we see man's fascination with the unfalsifiable.

It's interesting to note, that a deterministic worldview manifests these characteristics. Researchers in behavioral science performed experiments to determine whether a determinist worldview or a libertarian worldview came naturally to people, or whether either might be influenced by one's culture.

The experiment was done to kindergarten children from diverse cultural backgrounds. The scientist placed a folded cardboard box in front of a child, opened the box, reached her hand into the box, and then touched the bottom of the box with the child watching. The child was then asked, if the scientist's hand could have touched any other part of the box. The experiment was designed to evidence whether the child's natural worldview was deterministic or indeterministic.

The child answering that the scientist could only touch the part of the box which she did, would evidence a deterministic worldview. The child answering that the scientist could touch any part of the box she desired, would evidence a libertarian worldview.

In 100% of the cases, children from all cultures indicated the scientist could touch any part of the box she chose too. It was also suspected that the preponderance of people who assert a belief in a deterministic worldview, derive their belief from others who successfully persuade them into the belief, and in the vast majority of cases, the process is facilitated by some form of honored intellectualism, such as an ardently admired college professor persuading a student.

As children grow up, the concepts of one's consequences of choice, in obedience or disobedience, constantly reinforce a predilection towards libertarian free will. Libertarian free will is the *de facto* presupposition all persons assume in daily social interactions.

This then forces the one who tenaciously holds to a deterministic worldview to exercise the same neurological processes found within the unfalsifiable belief system. And enjoy the same air of superiority, intellectual prowess, and philosophical efficacies, with the accompanying endorphinal stimulations.

Non-Calvinists occasionally remark about how Calvinists exhibit compartmentalized thinking. On the one hand, a deterministic worldview is explicitly and forcibly defended as the only legitimate view. And then curiously, totally abandoned within normal daily social interactions, where libertarian free will forms the *de facto* basis for judgment in all matters concerning right and wrong.

One Arminian remarked: "The Calvinist is a curious creature. He is 100% Arminian in all matters of daily intercourse and justice, and 100% anti-Arminian in all matters of theology". His belief system forces him to halt between two opinions.

There will always be people who embrace a certain position so radically that no amount of evidence can ever change the mind. It is not uncommon for people to become so psychologically invested that anything that doesn't affirm the belief is rejected, discounted and rationalized away. This, more than not, reflects recognized idiosyncrasies of human cognition and our inability to consider any observation or argument, which casts aspersions on the sacred object. This has often been observed while presenting evidence to people tricked by paranormal con artists and mystic gurus.

People often respond with anger and resentment, as if the truth were robbing them of the cherished belief. The ability for the human mind to look at a large body of evidence and focus on the 10%, which can be interpreted so as to affirm the belief, while rationalizing away the 90%, which contradicts it, is a tribute to the way man is fearfully and wonderfully made. And it can also be noted as evidence that love is indeed blind.

It is illuminating to observe here another indicator of an unfalsifiable belief system. Successful "offensive" and "defensive" enunciations on its behalf require a perpetual evolution of ad hoc complexity by the addition of new, subtle and increasingly sophisticated distinctions, in order to make the system retain coherency and believability over time.

As such Calvinist enunciations become increasingly sophisticated and conceptually complex. Since that is the case, that Calvinists lament being misunderstood and misrepresented fits the pattern well. And keeping up with its ever-growing library of subtle nuances has been likened to chasing a greased pig.

Part 17. Partisanship identity—vicarious boastings—and the seductiveness of hero worship:

Kenneth Burke (1897), an American literary theorist, in Attitudes Toward History, writes: "In America, it is natural for a man to identify himself with the business corporation he serves. This is his birthright, and insofar as he is denied it, he is impoverished and alienated. But insofar as business becomes a 'corrupt sovereign', his only salvation is to make himself an identity, in an alternative corporation. The struggle to establish this alternative corporation is called the struggle for the 'one big union'. Hence, the drive for 'industrial unionism' for parties, farmers and workers, etc."

Burke is describing the sociological phenomenon of an individual's re-mapping of personal identity. From an insignificant persona, to an identity of preeminence by association with a group. Burke clues us, that 'vicarious boasting' is one of the outward manifestations to look for:

"One may note, however, the subtle ways in which identification serves as braggadocio. By it, the modest man can indulge in the most outrageous 'corporate boasting'. He identifies himself with some corporate unit (church, guild, company, lodge, party, team, college, city, nation, etc.) –and by profuse praise of this unit, he praises himself. For he 'owns shares' in the corporate unit — and by 'rigging the market' the value of the stock as a whole, he runs up the value of his personal holdings. We see the process in its simplest form, when the music-lover clamorously admires a particular composer, and so 'shares vicariously' in the composer's attainments. Such identification will be observable even among mistreated clerks of rival business concerns, as the sales girls of one department are somewhat contemptuous of the goods of the department store across the street (an attitude that the heads of the business are prompt to 'cash in on' by putting 'company loyalty' against interference from outside agitators and union organizers). The function of 'vicarious boasting' leads into the matter of 'epic heroism' and 'euphemistic' vocabularies of motives. When heroes have been shaped by legend, with the irrelevant or incongruous details of their lives obliterated, and only the most 'divine' attributes expressed, the individual's 'covert boasting' (by identification with the hero) need not lead to megalomania (extreme delusion of grandeur)….the legendary hero, is by definition, a superman. He is the founder of a line."

Not long ago, I watched a program on a Christian television channel noted for promoting Calvinism. The program contained a panel of Christians representing various segments of Evangelical Christianity, in response to increasing concerns over anti-Christian government policies.

There were no indicators of sectarianism at the outset, so I became interested in the discussion. The host, calmly and impartially, asked a single question of each member of the panel, eventually coming to the last member, at which point the host's demeanor suddenly changed, and his language approached effusive doting. I said aloud: "watch this…I'll bet this is Calvinist propaganda at work".

Sure enough, the host setup the last panel member, allowing him to launch into an embarrassingly prolonged idolization of Augustine, whom he called his 'home boy', inferring the answer to all of life's problems can be found in embracing Augustine and an allegiance to church. Of course, I understood his cloaked language for "church" meant Calvinism. The host went on, surreptitiously praising this one panel member, excitedly asking him to recommend book authors for the audience.

Now I know I'm witnessing classic Calvinism at work, and I scrambled to obtain a notepad and scribble the names of the suggested authors, to confirm my suspicions. Sure enough each one was a staunch Calvinist. I watched for signs of agitation or insult on the faces of the other panel members, during the embellished display, and didn't detect any. But the event fits the model of Calvinistic 'vicarious boasting' perfectly.

And I applaud Kenneth Burke for describing this behavior for us so wonderfully! Calvinists play this game continuously on public forums, being extremely careful not to let people know they are promoting Calvinism.

And this is what clues us in that they are operating surreptitiously. The Calvinist 'owns shares' in the corporate unit — and by 'rigging the market', assuming the role of an investment expert, he covertly sells dividends, seeking to induce buy-in on the stock. And by this process runs up the value of his personal holdings while secretly longing for a little vicarious hero worship himself.

Let us not be desirous of vainglory, provoking one another, envying one another;

Galatians 5:25. For brethren, you've been called into liberty. Only don't use your liberty for an occasion to the flesh, but by *agape*; serve one another. For all the law is fulfilled in one word: You shall agape your neighbor as yourself. But if you bite and devour one another, take heed that you are not consumed by one another;

Galatians 5:13 through 15. Beware of dogs— beware of evil workers— beware of the concision. For we are the circumcision, which worship God in the spirit, and (rejoice in Christ Jesus), and have no confidence in the flesh; Philippians 3 2 and 3. Nevertheless I have somewhat against you, because you have lost your first love. Revelations 2:4.

Every Christian group has its unique hierarchy of sins. Certain select sins are represented as grave and deadly, while others are systemically winked at, and some sins are actually lauded.

Within the society of Calvinism, hero worship is never categorized as carnality or sin. On a systemic basis, respecting of persons is used as a carrot on a string technique, and Christian youth are particularly vulnerable to its seductions. The Calvinist cannot praise himself and be perceived as spiritually minded, but he can get around this obstacle by the strategy, which Kenneth Burke in his insightful and apt descriptions, reveals as 'vicarious boastings'. And unwitting Christians are totally void of any ability to recognize how they are ensnared by the lure of hero worship.

Part 18. Don Quixote's two-headed windmill— Calvin's Gnostic dragon:

The story of Don Quixote follows the adventures of Mr. Alonso Quixano, who having lost sanity, and outfitted with a horse, knight's armor and lance, sets out to slay evil dragons, which ironically turn out to be windmills. Using highly rhetorical orations, the gallant one boldly boasts he will bring true divine justice to the world of chivalry and knighthood.

Ever since Calvin's writings became circulated and examined, antagonists have perennially pointed to a two-headed Gnostic dragon lurking deep within the system's dark underworld. One head of the fierce beast, breaths out ethical dilemmas from its inner belly, while the other billows out rational conundrums. Therefore, it is not uncommon, for us to observe, within any given generation, a Don Quixote or two, charging off, outfitted with shining philosophical armor, trying his gallant hand at slaying the formidable beast. We also note with Don Quixote's inflated knighthood, he carries the polished lance of inflated language.

Dr. William Lutz in "Doublespeak" writes: "Inflated language is a type of doublespeak, designed to make the ordinary seem extraordinary; to make everyday things seem impressive; to give an air of importance to people, situations, or things that would not normally be considered important; to make the simple seem complex. Calvinist Dr. James N. Anderson understands Calvin's two-headed problem, and gallantly sets out to try his hand at slaying the beast—with a theory he calls: "The authorial model of providence".

Unfortunately, what starts out as a theory, ends up looking more like fanciful imaginations. But the details of the theory are illuminating for us, as they affirm the existence of the system's ethical dilemmas and rational conundrums (i.e., its two-headed dragon). The idea seeks to assert a mystical, and unknown: "Divine Causation", which is not subject to scientific rational laws of logic, and is to be distinguished from what is called: "Intermundane" (relating to, or residing in the heavenly realm) causation.

Before we look at this, lets first recognize that secret-knowledge is a consistent element within unfalsifiable belief systems. If something is mystical, secret, and inscrutable, how is it the believer happens to know just enough about it to build an exegetical labyrinth around it? How is it that he conveniently knows just enough facts about the secret-gnosis, to urge us to believe what he asserts is the gospel, and then righteously scold enquiring minds who dare ask logical questions?

The story of Joseph Smith follows the same model, where it is asserted that he was shown the whereabouts of golden plates by a heavenly messenger named Moroni, and learned the secret-gnosis by being enabled to read hieroglyphic reformed Egyptian text. Likewise, the Da Vinci Code, asserts a secret-gnosis, which if revealed, could devastate the very foundation of Christianity.

Here Alpha-Causation is construed as a mystical, unknown form of causation, which doesn't conform to the universal laws of rational logic. Unknown to us before now: "Divine Causation, operates at a fundamentally different level than intermundane causation". Here, Divine Causation is also called Alpha-Causation, and intermundane causation; Beta-Causation. And further, Alpha-causation is likened to a human authoring a novel. The author can have characters in the novel doing hideous things, but since the author is not actually doing the hideous things himself, he is therefore not culpable.

It turns out, this idea is quite dated, and collapses quickly with the understanding that characters in a novel are not real but imagined, while Adam and Eve, were not imagined characters in a novel, but were real.

Dr. Anderson does acknowledge this fact. So then, are Alpha and Beta Causation real, or are they imagined within a novel idea?

Early in the paper, Dr. Anderson writes: "At some point in time for reasons we may never understand, Adam chose evil over good – he rebelled against his creator – and in so doing he corrupted human nature and his progeny." But later in the paper he writes: "Calvinists can affirm that there is a sufficient ultimate explanation for Adam's sin: God decreed it.

Indeed, there is a sufficient causal explanation: God Alpha-caused Adam's sinning but he didn't Beta-cause it. From there, he moves to the (*Argumentum Ad Ignorantiam*) argument, asserting: "We cannot simply assume that our natural intuitions about Beta-causation can be transferred without qualification to Alpha-causation."

But it hasn't yet been established, whether Alpha or Beta Causation are real or imagined. As was observed initially, the reason a human author would not be culpable for his characters actions is because the character doesn't exist. And since the character doesn't exist, culpability doesn't exist either. Additionally, if Adam is a character in God's novel, then Adam's sin is not logically necessary for the sake of the story line of the novel, unless it is a requirement based on a limitation of God's abilities.

Sin as a means to God's ends, is only logically necessary if God's abilities for achieving His ends are somehow limited. But mainstream Christianity holds that God is omnipotent, and therefore has no such limitations.

And Calvinists agree that God can create a world in which He causally determines all creatures to love and serve him without the need for sin. So, this line of reasoning, so far, appears somewhat contrived and its rational coherence questionable.

If God is the ultimate sufficient cause of every event, then the appeal to an intermundane causation is a puzzlement, as the understood laws of physical causation are effectively rendered unnecessary. And the concept of primary and secondary causes, are swallowed up by one single divine causal law, where all chains of events occur solely due to God's divine meticulous control over all events, no matter where each event occurs within a sequential chain.

It appears, what we have then is a form of mono-agency, where all entities, whether sentient or not, operate solely as instruments, where all creaturely movements are caused by supernatural energies of divine decrees. So then, on this view, since God is the sole cause and movement of Adams every faculty, any causation on Adams part is either non-existent, or is at least so impotent that it is causally irrelevant. How can Adam be held accountable when supernatural forces, which he has no ability to resist or alter, bring about his every neurological and physical movement?

Lastly, Dr. Anderson rules out "Beta-Causation" on Adams part, because Adam's internal state was holy good when he sinned. This leaves "Alpha-Causation" as the only possible causal force at work at the time. But if we follow Dr. Anderson's two assertions: (A) Adam is culpable for sin, and (B) "Beta-Causation" is ruled out; then we are left with the question of how Adam could have "Alpha-Caused" his own sin.

Additionally, since it is asserted the God Alpha-Caused Adam's sinning, then how can we rationally say that Adam is solely culpable? If however, the Calvinist can invent or discover a form of causation that defies all universal laws of logic; then that would be a different story. Perhaps in the future, such a causation will be discovered, and then persons can be successfully convicted for crimes they don't' have the ability to stop themselves from committing.

Here we see the two urgencies classically at work in the Calvinist. Firstly, he wants to assert God's absolute monarchical control of all things, totally extracting all possible causal ability from the creature, attributing absolute universal causal determinism solely to God alone. But he is then left with a two-headed (unethical and irrational) dragon, and the concern for the negative impact it will have on Calvinism's reputation and possible recruitment potential.

We observe that the labels Dr. Anderson uses, are more inventive than the more commonly used terms: "monergism" vs. "synergism", where it is often asserted that good events occur from God's causal activity as (monergistic events), and evil events occur from the combination of God's causal ability and man's causal ability as (synergistic events).

But even in the synergistic model, the Calvinist struggles providing any successful ethical or rational explanations for how God's causal role, asserted as unlimited in scope, is absolved, while man's role, forced upon him by necessitating supernatural decrees, is solely culpable.

Dr. Anderson concludes by stating, "At this point, I must confess that further answers escape me, and I find my self concurring with reformed theologians who concede that sin is intrinsically irrational, and the entrance of human sin in to the world is in many respects, shrouded in mystery".

At this point, the two-headed dragon is certainly smiling, happily lurking within the dark caves of the doctrine. But who knows, if some new Don Quixote in the far distant future, will come forth and actually slay the ancient beast.

In the meantime, what this provides for us is an affirmation of the system's two-headed issues: ethical-dilemmas and rational-conundrums. It also fits the model of irresolvable questions inherent within unfalsifiable beliefs. And we can also see how language facilitating plausible deniability becomes the last reliable defense.

Part 19. Sovereignty outweighs ethics:

So, then this view allows that distinctions be made on attributes of God, such as His ethics, His morality, His benevolence, His Love, His wrath… etc. All attributes except sovereignty have distinctions applied to them, which radically alter the scope of their application. But it cannot be allowed there be any distinctions applied to God's sovereignty. For sovereignty must never be compromised by any other attribute of God. For Calvin, God's world is one of monarchical absolutism.

David Bentley Hart writes: "Frankly, any understanding of divine sovereignty so unsubtle that it requires the theologian to assert (as Calvin did) that God foreordained the fall of humanity so that his glory might be revealed in the predestined damnation of the derelict, is obviously problematic, and probably far more blasphemous than anything represented by the heresies that the ancient ecumenical councils confronted."

Part 20. Calvinism's exegetical rules for the interpretation of scripture:

The scripture indicates that God desires that all men be saved. Calvinist's historically, following Calvin's line of reasoning assume that scripture must contain non-explicit distinctions in this regard. Those distinctions must control the way one interprets the text of scripture. Accordingly, distinctions based on philosophical rational are assumed unquestioningly, and especially upon scriptures which represent God's will concerning persons. Calvinists realize that such distinctions are not explicit in the text. They therefore must assert those distinctions using exegetical rules, which control the interpretation of the text without physically altering it. All correct interpretation of scripture must affirm the doctrine of Universal Divine Causal Determinism. Any interpretation that does not is heretical.

So, we observe that Calvinists have historically applied added distinctions to verses in scripture, which are applied as implicit distinctions, because in most cases, those distinctions cannot be explicitly observed within the text. Although Calvinists have been noted as altering definitions for Greek words, to make their meanings affirm Universal Divine Causal Determinism, they don't appear to be willing to physically alter the text of scripture.

And so, Calvinists have historically applied Calvinistic distinctions in an automatic fashion while reading the text. In other words, the added distinctions are automatically inserted into the text, within the mind of the reader, at the time the text is read.

Calvinist bible studies are ways of reinforcing this mental conditioning. One can argue that the practice is simply good exegesis. But it should be evident how easy it is to recognize a socialization process, in which readers are conditioned to read the text through the lens of distinctions they are taught to assume as true.

It eventually becomes automatic, and the reader is then completely convinced, the way he is taught to read the text is, in fact, the "plain reading" of the text. Additionally, Calvinist study bibles and books proliferate the Christian market, but are hardly ever, labeled or advertised as Calvinist materials—in order to proliferate their unique distinctions.

With the understanding that Calvinist exegesis is driven by a rule that stipulates all scripture must be interpreted so as to affirm Universal Divine Causal Determinism, and this rule requires adding distinctions into texts— some examples of the Calvinistic reading of 1 Timothy 2:4 follow:

> God (particularly) desires all men be saved, but
> not in such a way that God (universally) desires

all men be saved. This distinction is commonly called "particular salvation".

God (un-salvifically) desires all men be saved, but not in such a way that God (salvifically) desires all men be saved.

God (un-effectually) desires all men be saved, but not in such a way that God (effectually) desires all men be saved.

God (desires) all men saved, but not in such a way that God (wills) all men saved.

All scholars note the Greek word *thelei* in this verse, is used over 200 times in the New Testament and typically denotes "desire". Since this is the case, the Calvinist may make a distinction between God's desire and God's will, asserting that God (desires) all men to be saved, but does not (will) all men to be saved. But this argument flies in the face of His assertions that God conceives, determinatively causes, and meticulously renders certain, all events, which come to pass.

This argument is an excellent example where, in his attempt to establish God's unlimited sovereignty, he shifts to the extreme position of explicitly and forcibly asserting God's absolute universal meticulous control over every event, including every human impulse—but when faced with the logical consequences of that assertion, retreats to the opposite extreme, with arguments that work to obfuscate the very meticulous control he just previously asserted. When doublethink is fully assimilated in the mind, it occurs spontaneously and automatically without thinking.

On the one hand, Calvin asserts that whatever obtains is caused by: "God's good pleasure". So now we must consider God's "good pleasure" that person "P" is not saved, simultaneous with God's "desire" that person "P" is saved. And the Calvinist is forced to embrace yet another distinction between God's "desire" and God's "good pleasure", As-If God's "good pleasure" is out of synch with His "desire".

To paint a picture of a being who meticulously controls every atomic movement of every molecule in the universe, but then has desires that are out of synch with his pleasure, which are out of synch with his will, raises the specter of incoherency and grasping at straws.

William Lane Craig, in Four Views on Divine Providence, notes the regrettable position he sees the Calvinist consistently puts himself in: Highfield the Calvinist thinks that God's will is invariably done and nothing escapes his will, it follows that God wills moral evil and even causes it to occur. Given that that is impossible, there must be no moral evil... Incredibly, but consistently, Highfield... says, on page 67; 'if evil is that which God does not will and God's will is always effective, then evil can have no genuine and lasting being'... Highfield has to deny that people act sinfully.

Highfield seems to appreciate the difficulty in which this puts him, where he says: 'If evil is nothing in itself, how can there really be evil acts, events, or states of affairs? Does my position not imply that they cannot exist? To most people, this seems manifestly absurd. But if I admit that such things really exist and God's will is invariably done in and through them, how can I escape the charge that I am making God the doer of evil?' How, indeed? Highfield tries to break down a sinful action into various aspects, such as intention, deliberation, decision, exertion, and results... But Highfield recognizes that evil intentions do occur. He says, 'The doctrine of providence locates the evil aspect of human action, not in the created being of humanity and not in its final results, but rather in the sinfulness of a heart that is bereft of the knowledge of God and the love of God and neighbor. Sin is not God's creature. It has no positive existence, and the false images it projects can never be real'. Clearly this answer will not suffice. For in Universal Divine Causal Determinism, the intention, the deliberation, the decision, and the exertion are all caused by God to occur. God is therefore the source of evil. Highfield tries to escape this result by saying 'In evil acts, God's concurrence overcomes the evil in the act, not allowing it to be truly and lastingly realized but instead bringing good out of evil'. Alas, this is all to no avail: of course, God can bring a good result out of evil, but the evil intent and decision are not therefore somehow rendered morally neutral so that sin becomes an illusion".

What we see repeatedly is simply a two-phased approach of asserting Universal Divine Causal Determinism, on the one hand, but then being forced into the unfortunate position of having to equivocate and obfuscate aspects of that assertion in order to camouflage its objectionable consequences—in this instance, by asserting that evil is a projection of false images which can never be real. Removing the flowery language—evil is an illusion.

Gordon D. Fee, Professor Emeritus in New Testament Studies, is considered one of the world's leading experts in pneumatology and textual criticism of the New Testament. Dr. Fee's commentary on 1st Timothy 2:4 contains the following notes: The one clear concern that runs through the whole paragraph has to do with the gospel as for everyone ("all people," verses 1, 4 through 6, and 7). In this view, the phrase 'this is good' in verse 3 refers to prayer for everyone in verse 1, thus seeing verse 2 as something of a digression—albeit as before (1:12-17), a meaningful one.

The best explanation for this emphasis lies with the false teachers, who either through the esoteric, highly speculative nature of their teaching (1:4-6) or through its 'Jewishness' (1:7) or ascetic character (4:3), are promoting an elitist or exclusivist mentality among their followers. The whole paragraph attacks that narrowness.

Paul now returns to his main concern, prayers for all kinds 'for all people'. The reason? Because God wants all "people" to be saved. That is good, and pleases God--might, of course, refer to the content of verse 2. But the relative clause in verse 4 indicates otherwise. This is good, Paul says; that is, prayers 'for everyone' is good, and pleases God our Savior, precisely because the God who has saved us (our Savior) wants his salvation to reach all people.

Part 21. My doctrine is bible based—yours is not—A.K.A my dog is better than your dog:

Three Christian doctrines: the trinity, the incarnation, and the atonement, are widely recognized as influenced by both philosophical and biblical constructs, but are also peculiar to Christianity alone. The doctrine of the trinity, for example can be readily seen as having its roots in, and springing out of, scriptural texts, where man desires to compile applicable scriptures concerning the nature and relationship between the Father, Son, and Holy Spirit, and formulate a way of enunciating a comprehensive, balanced, and rational understanding.

In contrast, doctrines focused on the orbiting of planets, laws of the cosmos, or laws of causation (e.g., fate or predestination), fall under a different category, as they are not the urgencies of scripture. Such concerns are readily found in philosophical urgencies external to Christianity. Many theistic and non-theistic traditions, which are thoroughly extra-biblical or anti-biblical, entertain and dispute these doctrines.

Since this is the case, it is easy to see the factors, which influence bible interpretations on these issues, are powerful, yet represent extra-biblical, philosophical distinctions, which can—more than is recognized—control the reading of scripture, rather than the reverse.

Additionally, bible believers hold that scripture is a reflection of truth. Therefore, scripture will affirm what one holds to be true. If an individual is convinced that X is absolutely and infallibly true, that individual is willing to allow scripture affirm X.

If, however, an individual is convinced that X is false, that individual will not be willing to allow scripture affirm X because the scripture does not affirm falsehoods. So you will not find any Christians angrily insisting "the bible clearly teaches a moon made out of green cheese" anytime soon. Such an assertion would be seen as idiotic, or the Christian who insisted upon it mentally unstable. But this represents an unseen vulnerability to the bible believer.

If someone can convince you that X is infallibly true, they are bound to find, within the large volume of verses in the bible, texts that can be used to affirm X, and apply inventive exegesis to prove it. Once that is accomplished, they can argue their doctrine is 100%

biblical. Those under their influence may not be cognizant of philosophical and sociological forces at work in the reading of scripture, and are not psychologically predisposed to recognize agenda-based exegesis.

There is the case of the Galileo Affair, in the early 1600's, where theologians asserted that the scriptures clearly teach a Geocentric Aristotelian solar system. Galileo discovered with his telescope, the movement of planets could be more accurately understood by the model Copernican expounded, where the earth and planets orbit the sun.

This dispute could have been life threatening for Galileo, as he dared to question the process of exegesis used by the theologians. Galileo did not believe that X (a Geocentric system) was true. How then could the bible teach something that is false? While the theologians did believe X was true, and found verses and exegetical arguments to insist upon it. But Galileo recognized philosophical forces were driving the interpretation, which the theologians chose to deny.

Thus, the theologian puts the cart before the horse, asserting the bible is the source of the doctrine, when in fact an extra-biblical belief controls his interpretation. Therefore, anyone who asserts his doctrinal tradition as 100% biblical, while accusing its competitor of less, is simply manifesting his ignorance of these factors, or has fallen victim to a guild of exegetical magicians.

Scholar N.T. Wright, in *Justification*, whimsically writes: "Romans 9-11 has become the happy-hunting-ground for theories about predestination".

Bob Hill, author of *Calvinism Unmasked* writes: "Augustine agreed with the Manichaeans that a mutable God was totally unacceptable. In this conflict between the Platonic doctrine of immutability and the literal interpretation of Scriptures, what had to change? Augustine's answer was that the literal interpretation of Scripture had to change. For Augustine the plain narratives of Scripture had to be reinterpreted by spiritual or allegorical methods to agree with his philosophical presuppositions. The Manichaeans believed the Old Testament revealed a God who was mutable or could repent. Since the Platonists believed that God was immutable this idea of God repenting was a source of ridicule for the Catholic Church. Augustine was so embarrassed by these arguments that he chose to reinterpret Scripture rather than refute the Platonic philosophy."

Part 22. Listing a few Calvinist language techniques:

Since Universal Divine Causal Determinism is the lens through which the Calvinist sees God, along with a cosmos that entails dualistic morality, and since it inherently risks ascribing to God's conduct, the very evils, He declares He abhors, they perennially endure a backlash of shock, confusion, or disgust. These reactions affect Calvinism's reputation and evidence an observable hindrance to recruitment. In attempts to minimize this impact, a significant body of language techniques has evolved. Some of these techniques may include:

1) Cloaking causal terminology within ambiguous religious words

2) A high reliance upon words which can be interpreted as both universal and limited in scope

3) A high reliance on euphemisms to obscure the dark-side of the dualistic system

4) Framing concepts of benevolence as both universal and non-universal

5) Asserting "A" while abhorring not "A", then later asserting not "A"

6) Deploying eisegesis while claiming to abhor eisegesis

7) Designing ad hoc arguments in Greek grammar, which collapse under expert scrutiny.

8) Using eulogistic, religious language as an anesthesia, to numb the shock of glorified-evil

9) Vividly describing evil, while rejecting the common English labels for the evil described

10) Vividly describing evil, while inferring it good or necessary

11) Rejecting libertarian free will in man, while ascribing libertarian culpability to man

12) Framing God's causation as "active", then later framing the same causation as "passive".

13) Asserting other theologies as heretical, and then deploying their language to appear benevolent

Part 23. The language of marketing – benevolence and equivocations on selected terms:

Since Calvin's published works raised no small degree of discomfort, and in some cases, downright vitriol, he spent much time and the crafting of many words to defend and make his system as appealing as possible.

Today the highly sophisticated use of language within the society is universally recognized. And Calvinists have become a force to reckon with, in their superior abilities to craft language. Calvinism is certainly not alone in its strategic and expert use of language. We see the same linguistic skills in advertisements and seasoned politicians.

The reader is asked to consider taking a serious look at the underlying rhetorical strategies used by anyone who would posture as a representative of Christ or of scriptural doctrine. If something is to be postured as "biblical", certainly it would be enunciated using the same rhetorical honesty exemplified by the language of scripture. The Hebrew people could have easily equivocated and obfuscated in the narratives of King David taking Bathsheba and killing her husband, or Moses' disobedience at the waters of Meribah. But the scriptures do not follow a pattern of pulling semantic rabbits out of hats, and making blatant logical contradictions magically disappear, while claiming to abhor such things. If one seeks to make the claim of being biblical, one's language should at least meet the biblical criteria of linguistic honesty.

William Lane Craig in the book Four Views on Divine Providence, reflecting on his dialogs with Calvinist proponents within the work, remarks concerning this, and makes it his introductory statement.

He notes how Calvinist proponents consistently fall short of enunciating what he calls the "Radical Distinction" that is foundational within the Calvinist system; that of Universal Divine Causal Determinism. Dr. Craig does not expand further on that reflection, but it does beg the question; why it is consistently and historically the case, and whether it manifests a systemic marketing strategy of semantic under-specification.

The Calvinist has an intense urgency to market the product. But he knows his enunciations of God's causal role in evil events will elicit shock, consternation, or repulsion, all which backfire his efforts.

Calvinist language tends to be extremely reliant upon equivocations or evasions in five primary categories.

(1) Words or terms which reflect causation.

(2) Words or terms which represent God's disposition towards man.

(3) Words or terms reflecting God's relationship to evil.

(4) Words or terms having to do with salvation.

(5) Words or terms having to do with man's condition.

It should be easy to understand why these categories are of primary concern. But most non-Calvinists are simply not prepared for the large degree of marketing techniques, equivocations and evasions that proliferate the language. Once one understands why these categories are of primary concern for the Calvinist, being on the lookout, with due diligence, is certain to yield results in abundance.

Alan Greenspan was noted as saying: "If what I just said makes sense to you, then you probably didn't understand what I just said".

Ronald Reagan was noted for the saying: "Trust, but verify, verify, verify".

These are good things to remember as you attempt to deconstruct Calvinist language. Review every word, looking for hidden meanings, hidden presuppositions, irrationalities, and subtleties. Rhetorical trickery will be proportionate to the reputation of the author. But be advised that Calvinists of little reputation will often deploy language tricks designed by the masters. Once you become familiar with the general library of semantic tricks, you eventually gain an intuitive sense for spotting them.

Part 24. Compartmentalization of information— Outsider vs. Insider language:

It is wonderfully refreshing to see Calvinist's themselves identify the problems others see. We applaud Professor Dr. Paul Owen and thank him for being true to Christ. He writes the following: "People are sometimes surprised to hear me, A Calvinist, speak of the TULIP cult. What do I mean when I speak this way? By a cult, I mean a sect within the broad landscape of Christianity, which takes as its operating center some principle other than Christ crucified. This is certainly the case for the Young, Restless and Reformed. It is obvious that the operating center, which holds this movement together, is TULIP, and not the gospel of the cross. One gets the impression that their sense of identity is inseparable from their sense of superiority."

Steven Alan Hassan is a licensed mental health counselor with extensive knowledge on the practices of religious groups. One of the characteristics he helps people look for; he calls Outsider vs. Insider information. The group implements recruitment efforts for the obvious reasons. But the recruitment processes soon lead to the strategic use of subtle rhetorical practices, which fall under the heading of semantic under-specification. Group members are taught how to speak to outsiders who may be in opposition to the group, and how to speak to an outsider who may be potentially recruited. Hassan calls this outsider language.

Outsider language incorporates the use of semantic ambiguities of definition, and especially the tactic of semantic under-specification. What Hassan means is the recruiter simply doesn't tell the truth, the whole truth, and nothing but the truth when he speaks. Group members may be persuaded that God is blinding the eyes of the outsider so that he cannot understand the sacred doctrine.

The reality very will might be that the outsider recognizes elements of obfuscation and semantic discrepancies, but is not expert enough in the use of language or the doctrines of the group to recognize how and what semantic strategies the group typically deploys.

Group members may be convinced that since their doctrine represents the "gospel", and skillful linguistic tactics may be deemed honorable and a measurement of the intellectual prowess of the man. Even if there is no intent to be dishonest, the line soon becomes blurred and dishonesty becomes a necessary evil, which is then rationalized as honoring God and defending His truth. A long-term problem then becomes ambiguous language tactics deployed, and a conscience soon overpowered by a façade of righteousness.

Group members may become idolized based on their abilities to deploy slick biblical or logical sounding language, or posture speaking with authority. Sometimes little packs start to form by group members, reminiscent of dog packs, where a hierarchy and respecting of persons immerges based upon the intellectual or linguistic prowess of persons within the pack.

There is also the possibility that group representatives do not mean to be intentionally surreptitious, but as the group evolves, one of its hidden strengths becomes semantic magicianry. One of the most successful ways to tell a lie and not be detected is to simply divulge a limited amount of the truth. When a person tells a lie, there is the possibility of verifying its truth-value. But for that information which is carefully withheld, there is nothing to verify.

So, liars learn how to withhold information and fill in the missing gaps with connotative, religious, or moral-high-ground language, in order to give the appearance of providing honest, comprehensive or rational statements.

Part 25. Ambiguous terms and ad hoc definitions—shifting semantic landmarks:

In a court of law, those persons who have a critical role in the official dialog during proceedings, all work from one prescribed lexicon of words. "Agent" and "Instrument" have two distinctly different meanings, and the court strictly forbids them being conflated. "Freely" committing the crime, has a distinctly different meaning from "Caused" to commit the crime. And again, the court strictly forbids such terms from being conflated. "Permitted" to commit the crime, and "Caused" to commit the crime, are not to be conflated.

The reason for such lexical strictness should be self-evident. The court's urgency is the discovery of truth. Without truth, the word "Justice" is meaningless. Without "truth" the word "Holiness" is meaningless. Without "truth" the word "Righteousness" is meaningless. And the truth-value of everything we know or think we know hinges upon our definition of it.

When God commanded Noah to build an arc, or Moses to build the tabernacle, the process involved the use of words. These words, exchanged between God and man included words defining numerical values, and units of measure; as in "50 Cubits". We should easily recognize the critical nature of a commonly shared lexicon between persons. The building of a boat or a tabernacle could not be possible if God and man do not share the same exact meaning for all words used in the dialog.

Remove not the ancient landmark—Proverbs 22:8.

A just weight is God's delight—Proverbs 11:1.

Altered word definitions, especially concerning the things of God, should represent a significant warning-sign that something untoward is at work.

Part 26. Word games and the urgency to market the product:

A young man takes a girl up to lover's lane and she soon discovers his intent. As he reaches, she puts up her hand making a "Stop" motion. "Before we do this I need to know if you 'love' me" she says sternly. The young man knows what the girl's definition of the word "love" is. He knows she defines "love" as monogamous commitment. If he speaks honestly, and answers her question using her definition for the word "love", his answer will be "no". In such case, his quest will be foiled. So, he reasons within himself, that he must mislead her.

"Of course I love you" he says, and then fills in using language he knows she will trust— Argument by Emotive Language. But the caveat is; he won't tell her what "type" of love he has in mind. His strategy is another form of insider language. He knows what her definition for "love" is, but he creates an ad hoc definition for the word, and retains his definition as insider information. It should be clear to all that this is the language of marketing, cunning politicians, and religious recruiters.

Jerry Walls, a Scholar and Professor of Philosophy, gives a video presentation, which he calls "What's wrong with Calvinism". During the presentation Walls relates a situation in which young Calvinist pastors have asked an older Calvinist theologian and professor, if it would be honest for them to tell people that God loves them. Here it is visible that Calvinists themselves struggle with issues of linguistic honesty forced upon them by the system.

The theologian's response is illuminating, because it follows the same line of reasoning used by the young man at lover's lane. He assured them "Of-course you can tell them God loves them". But the caveat is; you can't tell them what [type] of love God has for them.

How would people respond, if you told them that the "type" of love God has for them, is the "type" of love that will throw them into a lake of fire for his good pleasure? It would be nice to tell them, the "type" of love God has for them is the "type" of love that is full of benevolence for them. But for a Jesus honoring Calvinist, that could not be honest. So, they are counseled to deploy benevolent sounding half-truths. That these young men couldn't see through such advise as dishonest, is evidence that the system teaches its adherents to become good at using slight-of-words tactics in order to make the product appear appealing and to achieve buy-in.

It is well understood that pharmaceutical companies, in order to market a product, will release results from laboratory tests, which would induce consumer buy-in, while withholding results which would make them avoid it. This is the classic "closed file cabinet" trick. Results from laboratory tests are carefully tucked away in the back of a file cabinet where no one will ever see them. The strategy is to make the product appear as appealing as possible while obfuscating its dangerous or distasteful characteristics. Jerry Walls concludes this phenomenon within Calvinism by stating: "If Calvinists did not resort to these types of misleading rhetoric, Calvinism would lose credibility in two years".

All of these evidences of Calvinist language games seem to point to a systemic compromise with ethics, in order to market the product. It raises the specter of a group, so radically biased, it is unable to recognize unethical tactics in its own midst, or whether the necessity for—

and rationalizations of—dishonesties, was long ago imbedded within its tradition.

Part 27. Calvinism's embrace of compatibilistic free will:

In philosophy, compatibilism is the assertion that free will and determinism are conceptually and logically compatible.

The compatibilist, for example, believes that it is possible for the thoughts, words and deeds of a human to be predestined in such a way as to be unavoidable and causally necessary, and yet be said to operate in accordance with a form of free will. The compatibilist asserts a definition of free will that is radically different from what is known as "libertarian" free will. The "libertarian" sense of free will is typically stated as the ability to refrain, or the ability to do otherwise, and includes alternate possibilities in life events. In other words, a person who perpetrated or participated in an event had the liberty and ability not to.

Compatibilists define free will as the freedom to act according to one's internal inclinations without external forces applied by another individual. In philosophy, compatibilism is a form of "Soft Determinism" and it is common by Compatibilists to view man as a machine, as one might view a high-precision clock. All of man's thoughts, words and deeds evolve through interactions, which occur internally, within the bio-mechanisms of the man. So it is in this way, man is said to function according to internal mechanical inclinations.

This is very similar to the concept of a man functioning as a highly complex biological machine, whose every thought word and deed are controlled by pre-defined software algorithms which are designed to reside internally within the biological mechanism.

Harry G Frankfurt (1929), an American philosopher, described compatibilism in terms of internal inclinations that may be antagonistic to one another. Frankfurt described these as "first-order" or "second-order" inclinations. Frankfurt asserted that the inclination, which ends up becoming dominant, represented the individual's "real-self", and therefore should be seen as an explanation for free will. The Compatibilist sense of free will is internationally categorized as a metaphysical distinction, and is rejected in aspects of English law.

Compatibilists may assert that the compatibilist form of free will can be present in non-metaphysical events. However, for legal precedence, a compatibilistic sense of free will is thought to undermine the ability to determine a person's causal role to an event. That is to say, justice requires the presumption that an individual could have done otherwise than he did.

The terms *Mens Rea* and *Actus Reus* developed within English Law represent principles in which a general test of guilt requires proof of fault, culpability, or blameworthiness both in thought and action. For example, person "A" shoots person "B", while having an epileptic seizure, would not meet the *Mens Rea* mental requirements for legal culpability, and an airplane being blown off course into a foreign country's air-space would not meet the *Actus Reus*, action requirements for legal culpability. A few other examples of common distinctions include: "voluntary" man slaughter, in regard to murder, and "of sound mind" in regard to a will and testament. The "libertarian" sense of free will must first be established within the body of evidence as proof of culpability, and in most cases is assumed.

Compatibilism was first observed in the writings of the Greek stoics of Augustine's period, and later in medieval scholastics. Ricardo Salles, author of God and Cosmos in Stoicism, writes "The stoics were determinists insofar as they maintained that every state or event is necessitated by prior causes; but, at the same time, they were Compatibilists since they were willing to defend the thesis that prior necessitation does not make impossible that we deserve praise or blame for actions we perform. So, the stoics were intent on proving that despite determinism, humans are genuinely responsible for their actions."

The distinction of compatibilistic free will is still the prevailing philosophical view among Calvinists, some cognitive scientists, such as Daniel Dennett (1942), some existentialist philosophers, such as Frithjof Bergmann (1930), and some Muslim scholars, such as Muḥammad Abduh (1849).

Calvinist theologian and philosopher, Jonathon Edwards, in The Freedom of the Will writes: "It most certainly is the case that God is in that manner the disposer and orderer of sin, is evident to anyone who puts any credit in the Bible, as well as being evident because it is impossible in the nature of things that it should be otherwise."

Edwards obviously embraces the systems underlying presupposition of Universal Divine Causal Determinism. He argues that whatever a divine being does must be unquestionably considered right, and that the creature is in no position to question such things. Philosophers view Edwards as an advocate of compatibilistic free will in defense of Calvinistic distinctions. He additionally asserts that even though God moves every human faculty, humans are still to be considered agents and not mere instruments.

It is questionable whether Calvin was familiar with the distinctions of compatibilism vs. libertarianism, because in his writings Calvin consistently swings back and forth between the two opposing (non-libertarian / libertarian) conceptions of free will in his arguments. Rejecting libertarian free will in one argument, and then requiring it in the next. In those instances, in which Calvin is intent upon asserting God's sovereignty or relationship to good, Calvin firmly and explicitly argues from a non-libertarian and fully deterministic position. Additionally, Calvin may often cast harsh dispersions upon any libertarian concept of man's will as hideous nonsense.

However, when Calvin is intent on eulogizing God's role in sin or evil and holding man solely culpable for the things God meticulously makes him do, Calvin relies upon the very libertarian free will he just rejected, in order for his argument to appear coherent.

Calvin's consistent trading back and forth on two opposing concepts of free will, points to two possibilities; that he was confused, and conflated the two concepts, or he was equivocating causal terminology in an attempt to make both arguments look coherent.

Essentially Calvin argues:

> (1) God is the sole causal agent in all events and gives man absolutely no alternative possibilities for function or faculty.

> (2) Man is solely responsible for sinful/evil things God makes him do.

(3) God is solely responsible for good things
God makes man do.

Ever since modern philosophers took up the distinction
of compatibilistic free will, Calvinists have valued it, as
it supports the deterministic foundation of the doctrine.
However, it can present additional temptations for
dishonesty in their recruitment efforts. When a
Calvinist is enunciating Calvinistic distinctions to a
mainstream Christian, it is not unusual for them to be
asked if they reject free will. Without realizing it, the
mainstream Christian is asking if the Calvinist believes
in "libertarian" free will.

The Calvinist may often take advantage of this dialog,
as he understands the distinction of deterministic
Compatibilistic free will vs. libertarian free will, while
the mainstream Christian does not. So, the Calvinist can
respond with: "of course we believe in free will". What
he withholds however is what "type" of free will he has
in mind. So again, we are back to the linguistic strategy
of the young man at lover's lane and the use of insider
language.

You can imagine what a person's response would be
when told the "type" of free will the Calvinist has in
mind, is one in which God conceives, decrees, and
meticulously renders certain that a person will choose
damnation and a lake of fire for eternity.

Calvinists are well aware that mainstream Christians would find that "type" of free will appalling. And so equivocating on causal terminology in order to obfuscate the system's "Radical Distinction", is all too often the natural and human thing to do. Consequently, the combination of their urgency to propagate, and the common negative receptivity to its dark elements, drives them to use misleading, obfuscating and benevolent sounding language, in order to make the system appear appealing to the unsuspecting.

Part 28. Major Points of contention within philosophical disputes over determinism:

Peter van Inwagen (1942), a Christian analytic philosopher, in *The Consequence Argument* writes: "If determinism is true, then our acts are the consequences of the laws of nature and events in the remote past. But it is not up to us what went on before we were born, and neither is it up to us what the laws of nature are. Therefore, the consequences of those things, including our present acts, are not up to us."

A brief review of the points of contention, which perennially orbit around the philosophies of determinism vs. indeterminism, can be sited as questions concerning:

1. The existence of libertarian free-will

2. The sacrifice of ethics and morality in deference to utilitarian power

3. Man as an instrument rather than an agent

4. A conception of man operating simply by pre-designed mechanical inclinations, i.e., a robot.

It is no surprise to observe these are, in fact, same exact points of contention between Calvinism and its alternatives, once one realizes the system is founded upon the often-invisible element of causal determinism.

One could conceivably differentiate those components within Calvinism, whose source can clearly be traced to Christianity, apart from those components whose source can clearly be traced to the philosophy of causal determinism. And to additionally consider the component of causal determinism as the primary cause of contention between Calvinism and its alternatives. As has been noted, all of the major points of contention, which have orbited around perennial debates between Calvinists, are the same exact points of contention, which have perennially orbited around debates between determinists and non-determinists in the field of philosophy.

It is interesting to consider the scurrilous and contentious arguments and almost hateful emotions that so often accompany disputes which have occurred between Christians over one single issue, and how that issue may in fact, not be an issue of scripture, but rather an issue of philosophy. Obviously, the affect that determinism and non-determinism has had on human concepts of the nature and character of God, and the world in which He has created, cannot be understated. Just as nature abhors a vacuum, all philosophical propositions inherently produce logical consequences.

Part 29. Compatibilistic responsibility vs. Libertarian responsibility—halting between two opinions:

In this section I hope to forward a line of reasoning that both the Calvinist and non-Calvinist can acknowledge; having to do with the elements of free will and responsibility; often called "moral responsibility".

Firstly, it is commonly acknowledged that free will in any form comes with some form of responsibility. All parties, (i.e., Calvinists and non-Calvinists) hold that man has some form of free will, along with its associated moral responsibilities. Since Calvinism is founded upon theological causal determinism, Calvinists have quite naturally embraced a compatibilistic form of free will, while the non-Calvinist, who is an indeterminist, holds to a libertarian form of free will.

Secondly, all parties hold that compatibilistic free will, on man's part, is a free will, which is causally determined by God, and that God, in the exercise of his sovereignty over all states of affairs, which obtain, does not allow alternate possibilities, beyond what he determines to obtain.

On this view, for example, man has a free will in which a certain human function can obtain, but whatever specific human function obtains, does so because God causally determines that specific function to obtain. And as such, no other alternative function can possibly obtain. And so it follows that the compatibilistic form of free will is acknowledged as a (limited) form of free will, (as it pertains to human faculties), by virtue of the fact that God does not allow any alternative possibilities outside of what he causally determines to obtain.In other words, man is not at liberty to exercise whatever faculty he chooses (which would be true in libertarian free will), because God solely causally determines every human function or faculty that will obtain.

Thirdly, all parties would acknowledge that God himself has free will. And generally this would be sited as a libertarian form of free will, because, as we have seen, the libertarian form of free will is not limited, as the compatibilist form of free will is. This is to say that God is free to will as many alternate possibilities as are logically possible for him to choose. And since God's free will is not causally determined by any outside entity, person, or antecedent event, His free will does not have the limitations that we observe within a compatibilistic form of free will imposed upon man.

Now we must point out at this time that some things are not possible for God. For example, let's say that God wants to causally determine that a certain event, which we will call event "positive E" will obtain. And let us also say that it is possible for God to causally determine an alternative event, which we will call event "negative E" to obtain. And let us further say that event "negative E" is the exact negation of event "positive E". Now we see that either event is possible for God to cause to obtain. But it is not logically possible for God to make both events obtain at the same time, because one event will negate the other.

And in such case, neither event will obtain. It is assumed that all parties will acknowledge that God is not illogical, making two opposing events occur in such a way that both events negate each other. In other words, it is not possible for God to negate Himself. And as such, it is not logical, and therefore possible, for God to negate what he wills to obtain. Or further, it is not logically possible for God to be both God and not-God.

So far, we have identified three conceivable forms of free will:

1. God's free will

2. Man's compatibilistic free will

3. Man's libertarian free will

Now since all parties acknowledge that all forms of free will entail some form of moral responsibility, we can then acknowledge that each of the three forms of free will identified, have their own perspective form of moral responsibility. Now let us sight some examples of how each form of free will and its associated responsibility may interact with each other in human events which God causes to obtain.

In the case that a human baby is born, we have a human event. In such an event, it would seem evident, (all parties would acknowledge), a newborn baby cannot be held responsible for the selection of its mother, through whom it is born. All parties would hold that the choice of the infant's mother is exclusively God's to make. God determines what babies will be borne to what mothers, and that is God's choice exclusively. Therefore, it should be acknowledged that the associated responsibility that would come with that choice is solely God's. Another way to say this is that the infant has 0% choice, and 0% responsibility in choosing its mother. And that God has 100% choice along with 100% of the responsibility for choosing what mother will birth a given infant.

So we see that there are human events, which God causes to obtain, in which He bears 100% of the responsibility. We have already established that during a compatibilistic free will event, God only allows that which he has determined to obtain.

Now let us say God causes a human to think a certain thought, and let us call that event [DCT] (divinely caused thought). This type of free will event, (as it pertains to the human) constitutes a limited form of free-will, exercised by the human. But there is no such limitation in God's exercise of His free will in causing "DCT" to obtain.

Now it certainly would seem implausible that any party would deny that God, exercising His free will, in causing event "DCT" to obtain, would not rightly assume the associated responsibility that is proportionate with that free will which God has exercised. In other words, no party would assert that God exercises His free will irresponsibly. Therefore, since we acknowledge that God assumes his form of free will responsibility, and if man assumes his form of (limited) free will responsibility, it would follow that the percentage of responsibility which man would rightly assume, would be rightly proportionate to the (limited) form of free will man is allowed to exercise. And conversely, that the percentage of responsibility that God will rightly assume, will likewise be rightly proportionate to the (less limited) free will He exercises.

We might consider it highly difficult to ascertain the exact proportion of responsibility, which God would rightly assume in event "DCT", compared to the proportion of responsibility, which the human should rightly assume. But since we acknowledge that within event "DCT", man's free will is limited in a way that God's free will is not, it wouldn't seem logical or ethical to claim that the percentage of responsibility that man should rightly assume would represent 100%, since that would represent a false-balance, and disproportionate to the (limited) form of free will allotted to man, compared to the (less limited) form of free will exercised by God. If man's form of free will is significantly limited within his exercise of event "DCT", compared to God's form of free will in causing it, could we rightly claim that man bears the bulk of the responsibility?

It would seem that making such a claim would put us dangerously close to asserting a false-balance, which we understand through scripture, God abhors. Rather than place ourselves in a position of operating in something that God would abhor, it would seem prudent for us to simply allow man to assume that burden of responsibility that is rightly proportionate to his (limited) form of free will, and honor God by acknowledging, He will rightly assume that burden of responsibility that is rightly proportionate to His (less limited) form of free will.

Let us now contrast event "DCT" (divinely caused thought) with an event in which God allows man to have a thought within a libertarian free will state of affairs. Let us call this next event "NDCT" (i.e., non-divinely caused thought). In the "NDCT" event, God does not cause the man to have any specific thought. Man is given the liberty of having his own thoughts, which includes the liberty to refrain from a given thought.

In this state of affairs then, God does not limit man's free will or alternate possibilities, as God does in the causally determined state of affairs. Since it is the case that in this state of affairs, man's exercise of "NDCT" is less determined by God, and more determined by himself than it is within the causally determined state of affairs, it then follows that in this case, man's responsibility for "NDCT" would be rightly proportionate to the type of free will exercised. If God in this case refrains from causally determining "NDCT" to obtain, than we should honor God by acknowledging that He will rightly ascribe the right proportionate or percentage of responsibility to Himself for this event.

It would seem unethical to ascribe a high percentage of responsibility to God for "NDCT" than God would ascribe to Himself in the previous causally determined case. In this libertarian free will case then, it would seem ethical and just for us to ascribe the preponderance of responsibility to man, as God has allotted him a proportionally freer form of free will to exercise.

It would seem unethical and a false-balance for us to assert that in a causally determined state of affairs, God causally determines every human function in such a way as not to allow any alternative possibilities, and then ascribes to Himself absolutely no responsibility for His exercise of free will in such an event. For us to assert such a thing would seem to seriously dishonor God and risk operating in a false-balance which God would abhor. Certainly, we would want to honor God by both acknowledging that He rightly assumes His portion of responsibility for the free will He exercises, and additionally we would want to refrain from promoting a false-balance, which we know He would abhor.

Therefore, I would suggest that for either party to ascribe all of the responsibility to man, for those functions which God causes to obtain, and allows no alternative, would, in fact, constitute a false-balance, as well as seriously dishonor the good name of a righteous God, who is perfect in all His ways.

Part 30. Hyper-Calvinism—Sacrificial Straw Man or simply a Hard Determinist:

The "Sacrificial straw man" is a trick designed to distract people's attention from distasteful aspects of one's theory. It works firstly, by fabricating a fanatical version, then secondly shooting that version down, giving the appearance of distancing oneself from the fabricated extreme, in order to fabricate the appearance of balanced moderation. It is used to obfuscate the radical distinctions of one's system. We find this trick used by wine retailers, who strategically locate a few exorbitantly priced bottles amidst the others on display. It consistently works to manipulate the unsuspecting consumer, who will naturally gravitate to a median priced item.

People want to avoid appearing extreme—not too cheap—not too wealthy, so they will select bottles in the median-price range. With a few $100 bottles strategically located, the mean distribution of purchases will approximate $30, whereas if the $30 bottle were the most expensive items, the mean distribution would approximate $10 to $15 purchases. So we can see the strategy works to manipulate people by taking advantage of common human egocentric idiosyncrasies.

As has been stated, in ongoing debates held between philosophers concerning determinism, compatibilism is the view that determinism and free will are logically consistent. We then find that Compatibilists are at odds with In-Compatibilists, who come in two forms: Libertarians (i.e., indeterminists) and Hard Determinists. Compatibilism is then also at odds with Hard-Determinism. Hard Determinists totally deny free will in any form and hold to a cosmos, which is completely deterministic.

The terms "Hard Determinism" and "Soft Determinism" were coined by William James, (1842), an American philosopher psychologist, and libertarian who held compatibilism in disdain. James criticized compatibilism asserting it offered a "kinder-gentler" picture of determinism, which he held in strong contempt stating: "Now days there is a softer view of determinism, which abhors harsh words, and attempts to repudiate necessity, by simply calling it freedom." James felt Compatibilists were superficial and called their arguments "a bag of verbal tricks which they deploy as a way to avoid the real intellectual problems of free will", and "the entire compatibilist enterprise is a quagmire of evasion". He felt that Compatibilists were trying to avoid the reality of a deterministic world, with semantic tricks and verbal sleight of hand.

The German philosopher, Immanuel Kant (1724), held to a similar view, calling compatibilism "a retched subterfuge". What is more interesting is that both James and Kant felt that the Hard Determinists were the honorable and intellectually honest ones, who faced the problems of determinism and free will head-on, calling them "worthy adversaries". In fact many in philosophy today hold that compatibilism is the product of wishful thinking, and of wanting to have the best of both worlds, i.e., the benefits of determinism and the responsibility of libertarian free will, at the same time. So within philosophy, the Hard Determinist holds that determinism is true, and free will in any form is simply an illusion.

There are two components typically sighted within Hard Determinism. Hard Determinists reject compatibilism, asserting that Compatibilists do not want to face the logical implications of free will adequately. But while they feel that the libertarian definition of free will is the only logical definition, they also insist that free will in any form does not really exist. This view is then sometimes called the "error view" or "free will eliminativism", because the Hard Determinist is convinced that the notion of free will is simply a cognitive error, and mankind should eliminate the notion altogether.

So then, the Soft Determinist's view of the Hard Determinist is that he is a "Hyper" Determinist who takes things too far. While the Hard Determinist's view of the Soft Determinist, is that he is not willing to bite the bullet and be intellectually honest.

This polarization within the philosophy of determinism may also have its parallel within Calvinism. Since Calvinism is based upon the doctrine of Universal Divine Causal Determinism, it would be easy to assume, the same two types of determinists exist within the Calvinist fold. Many times, when defending themselves against criticism, Calvinists will insist that what is being depicted of them is an aberrant form of Calvinism called "Hyper" Calvinism.

It is true that the preponderance of Calvinists are Soft Determinists. And so, they often urge non-Calvinist critics to cease their criticisms, asserting the real culprits as the "Hyper" ones among them. However, to date, no Calvinists have come forward, actually declaring themselves as "Hyper". Therefore, within the population of Calvinists, those who are the "Hyper" ones, appear to be as elusive as the famed big foot.

It is speculated then, that "Hyper" ones exist within Calvinism, but it is hard to prove, as none are willing to publicly self-identify with the pejorative label ascribed by their clan.It does seem to be understandable; that just as there are different persons within philosophy, each assuming his individual position on the continuum-of-determinism, (i.e., a line which stretches between Soft Determinism and Hard Determinism), that this would also be reflected within the society of Calvinists. However, there are also no known books published by Calvinist authors who seem willing to identify as "Hyper". And this brings to light another problem.

With the evident illusiveness of the "Hyper" ones in their midst, those Calvinists who are frequently noted as rejecting "Hyper" Calvinism, do in fact produce a significant body of literature, in which Calvinistic concepts are defined in the very forms which they decry as "Hyper". And this phenomenon makes observers wonder if the "Hyper" Calvinist is, in fact, a fabricated straw man who doesn't really exist.

It may also be the case, that certain Calvinists, who interact in internal debates within their own society, do self-identify as "Hyper" or perhaps rather see themselves as the intellectually honest ones, who take Calvinism to its logical conclusions. If such Calvinists do in fact exist, we may also assume how readily they understand the negative reactions their "Hyper" enunciations would produce. And in order to therefore advance the cause — promote the system — increasing the surplus Calvinist population — are careful to keep their "Hyper" form of Calvinism behind closed doors where it is least likely to cause trouble.

Part 31. Jacob I love—Esau I hate—Calvinism's petri dish, of the Westboro Baptist kind:

It has often been noted, that one extreme benefit that Catholicism provides to Christianity, is its unabashed representations of religiosity and debauchery.

Over the centuries, Catholic authorities have occasionally become so brazen; they felt no need to obfuscate or hide anti-Christian, pagan sentiments. And in this regard, the Catholic Church seems to provide and endless supply of examples for the discerning Christian. There is, for example, the well-known statement by Pope Leo X: "How well we know what a profitable superstition this fable of Christ has been for us and our predecessors." Leo's blessed pronouncement is recorded in the diaries and records of both Pietro Cardinal Bembo (Letters and Comments on Pope Leo X, 1842 reprint) and Paolo Cardinal Giovio (De Vita Leonis Decimi, , op. cit.).

Later, to minimize negative impact, ministers of spin, attempted damage control; with the very semantic evasions and doublespeak we are now studying. They asserted the: "you don't understand us" argument, insisting the Pope had been misunderstood. When he used the word "profitable", he didn't mean it by its common definition, but what would be better understood as: "gainful". Likewise, when he used the word "fable", he didn't mean it by its common definition, but what would be better understood as: "tradition". But these attempts at semantic word games have been received with incredulity, since, in the same way a woman proudly displays her jewelry, the Catholic Church has, in so many ways, vaunted her pagan adornments.

Since the Catholic Church manifests its bacterium so clearly and unashamedly, the system serves as a rich textbook of maladies. As the physician studies symptoms of various diseases represented within medical textbooks, to best recognize them in future patients, one can study the various indicators and symptoms within Catholicism, which will later appear within other religious bodies. In this regard, the

Catholic Church has provided a veritable petri dish, readily available for ongoing examination.

Calvinism likewise, has its petri dish, and one of its more interesting life forms, appears at the Westboro Baptist Church, located in Topeka Kansas. This little church was established on the east side of Topeka. Fred Phelps, (1929), at age 17, attended Bob Jones University for two years before dropping out, citing racial issues as the reason for his departure. It is alleged, former college employees told the Topeka Capital Journal that Phelps had been given an ultimatum to seek psychiatric care or be expelled.

Phelps was a Calvinist of the most serious kind, insisting as Calvin did, that all sins committed by men come about by the impulses of God. The Westboro church initiated its first service with Phelps as pastor in 1955.

In a 1994 story in The Topeka Capital-Journal, Phelps sons, Nathan and Mark, said their father used the pulpit to vent his rage, and that he beat his wife and children with his fists, or the handle of a mattock to the point of bleeding. Shortly after becoming Westboro's pastor, Phelps broke ties with nearby Baptist congregations, and renamed the church using the term "Primitive Baptist".

The terms: "Primitive Baptist" or "Primitive Christian", often serve as cloaked language for Calvinism, especially during a church's infancy, in its attempts to maximize recruitment potential. Other terms such as "Grace Assembly" also work as code names for Calvinist congregations. Cloaked names help attract people who would otherwise avoid a Calvinist assembly.

The Westboro group averaged around 40 members—a little over the norm for a Calvinized congregation. Calvinists interpret Christ's statement that **"few** will enter in" to mean that God only elects few individuals as vessels of honor for salvation, while electing the remaining "many" as vessels of wrath. Therefore, it is common for Calvinist groups to be small in number, averaging around 20 persons, mostly in the form of families. Although pastor Phelps and the Westboro group do not self-identify as "Hyper", they have been denounced by the Baptist World Alliance and the Southern Baptist Convention as such.

Due to a glorified-evil dualistic, and deterministic worldview, we can see that Calvinists are faced with the same consternations within their internal sub-groups that exist between mainstream Christianity and Calvinists as a whole.Pastor Phelps and the Westboro group eventually became widely recognized throughout the U.S. for hate speech, especially against Gays, Jews, and various politicians. And the Anti-Defamation

League and the Southern Poverty Law Center have also similarly sighted them.

Westboro Calvinists are noted for their aggressive public activities, heavily involved in picketing, carrying signs displaying messages such as "Thank God for 9/11", "Thank God for IEDS", "Thank God for dead solders", and "God hates fags".

Libby Phelps Alvarez, the granddaughter of pastor Phelps states that she was born and raised in the group, but eventually left, after questioning its doctrines and practices. One of the issues Libby questioned concerned the practice of praying for the deaths of outsiders. Libby and her brother Nathan both acknowledge, they believed in, and participated in the group, because of its effective indoctrination practices.

Lauren Drain, was brought into the group at the age of 14, by her father while in his custody. In her book Banished – surviving my years in the Westboro Baptist Church, Lauren identifies the group as exhibiting the characteristics of a cult, and asserts the group exercised psychological control over its members, similar to what we find described by Robert J Lifton (1926), an American psychiatrist—as "Thought Reform".

Shirley Phelps, the daughter of Fred Phelps, after having also left the group, lamented on television, that a whole generation of her children are emotionally and psychologically scared as a byproduct of the group.

Megan Phelps-Roper, another granddaughter who also left the group, likens the group's dynamics to that of Jihadists, with a Taliban like theocracy. She cites the fact that the group insisted upon the eternal torment of outsiders based upon their conduct, but would not apply the same reasoning for persons within the group who were involved in similar sins. This began to bother Megan, and she eventually dared to question it.

The group's teachings sternly condemn persons to eternal damnation based on conduct, despite the logical contradiction that God meticulously, causally determined those person's conduct. But this was not the case for group insiders whose sins were declared forgiven. A controversy arose when Megan asked what would happen if an outsider repented. She was scolded and told outsiders were all damned for eternal torment because God would make sure they could not repent. Megan remembers a televised documentary reporter being told things like: "God is going to enjoy flicking you into a lake of fire". It was these logical and ethical conundrums, which eventually jolted Megan to her senses and compelled her to leave.

Megan also reflected, Westboro was "ISIS like", recalling an article she read in the New Yorker magazine in 2015, titled "Journey to Jihad--why are teen-agers joining ISIS". She relates how the Westboro group's reading of scripture was identical to the reading of the Quran she observed with the Jihadist group "Sharia for Belgium".

Another characteristic paralleling the religion of Islam was its public insistence that the deaths of Belgium police and politicians were the "punishment of Allah", or in the case of Westboro, the "punishment of God". And yet, she also recalls the goodness of God that she saw displayed between family members in the group.

It would appear that what Megan is reflecting on, is in fact, the glorified-evil, dualistic system. Megan describes her life as a teenager; walking outside the high school she attended, to picket the school during her lunch breaks, reflecting a form of doublethink. There was also a prevalent "Insider/Outsider" mindset that Megan sighted as a very strong characteristic, stating: "A frequent teaching in the group was you are either a Jacob or an Esau….God loved Jacob and hated Esau before they were born".

Megan left the group when she was 27. Although she is not willing to label the group a cult, she does acknowledge what she calls: cult-like indicators: group-think, group-identity, and selective-empathy. Megan states: "The stronger your identity as an insider in the group grows, the more you are able to suppress empathy for outsiders, and this biased suppression of empathy is reinforced as group members experience collisions with outsiders, increasing antagonism against them."

She further states: "The indoctrination. It's all or nothing. There can be no difference of opinion, no matter how slight, in matters of conscience within group members. When you are a member of a group, where your whole life is tied up in it, the threat of excommunication can be hung over your head."

Using Westboro as a textbook case, what we see then, are the socialization processes that are consistent within Calvinistic groups, where there is milieu control, a high emphasis on "elect" status, and a high emphasis on group conformity and unanimity.

Many Calvinists strongly deny association with what they site as a radical fringe. While, conversely many Calvinists see themselves as the true believers, and other Christians as compromised—and defend the Westboro group as "good Calvinists all".

Our vantage point in all this is that it provides a view of Calvinism's petri dish and a textbook view of the same systemic symptoms within all who take their Calvinism seriously. The same exact tenor, tone and topics of disputations occur between Calvinists and outsiders that exist with the Westboro group, howbeit obviously, in less extreme form.

But Calvinist controversies, whether they manifest enlarged, (Westboro style), or in miniature, are in fact due to the same underlying elements of a good-evil dualism and Universal Divine Causal Determinism, and the Calvinist petri dish is thus informative for the discerning Christian.

Part 32. Calvinist disputation techniques—the bullfighter, the carrot, the wolf pack, the snowflake:

The Calvinist's continuum line of determinism was previously mentioned. It is wise to understand how this works within the ranks of Calvinists.

Since Calvinism is founded upon the presupposition of Universal Divine Causal Determinism, and since that presupposition inherently entails God having a direct determinative causal role in evil, each Calvinist is forced to deal with the dark implications that are inherent within the system. And each Calvinist does that in his own unique way.

This can be likened to the Calvinist finding a comfortable location on a line. The line is the continuum-of-determinism, where one extreme end of the line points to indeterminism, and the other extreme end points to hard determinism.

Within the Calvinist society, the Calvinist who locates himself at the extreme Hard Determinism end, may well be sighted as "Hyper". Using a bell-curve representing standard deviation, the preponderance of Calvinists are going to reside as close to the indeterminist side of the line as possible, while still retaining an emphasis on sovereignty which would tend to pull them up the line towards Hard Determinism. So, understanding how each Calvinist embraces and retains his conscience on the line of determinism allows us to predict his representations of Calvinism.

Bullfighting is a traditional spectacle, and highly entertaining in various parts of the world. What we want to look at here, are a few illuminating aspects of this sport, and how it applies to dialogs with Calvinists. If you have ever seen bullfighting on television, at the onset of the event, where the bull and the man face each other, you probably have been struck by the significant contrast between the two parties. The bull is a huge mass of muscle and power, and quite often the bullfighter, a tall skinny looking, and string bean of a man. The contrast of power in this spectacle is quite impactful. The man is reliant upon the bull's limited intelligence. He positions himself, usually standing behind his bright red cape and imitates the body language of aggression, to which he knows the bull will respond. The bull charges the cape, thinking he is charging the man. The man then steps to the side of the cape, so the bull is unwittingly, no longer charging the man, but the cap. As the bull reaches the cap, usually with head down, in full charge, the man simply flicks the cap out of the way and the bull is left charging thin air. This process then repeats itself, and the bull is not intelligent enough to know how the strategy works.

This sport can occur between a Calvinist and interlocutor.

The Calvinist may assert the interlocutor is not qualified to critique Calvinism, because he doesn't understand it. The Calvinist hopes he can simply dismiss the interlocutor out of hand with this charge, or become an unwitting bull. Here we have the shaking of the red cape to confront the bull. If the interlocutor is unprepared for this technique, he unwittingly becomes an entertaining bull. At this point, the interlocutor interprets the assertion as a challenge to accurately enunciate Calvinism. If the interlocutor is unaware of the underlying presupposition of Universal Divine Causal Determinism, which functions invisibly within the system, (and we can now see how valuable its invisibility is to the Calvinist), the interlocutor has lost the game from the onset.

He is charging full speed into a red cape, assuming the role of an unwitting bull. In many cases the Calvinist's challenge, is itself a misleading statement reliant upon ambiguity. The interlocutor thinks the Calvinist is asserting he doesn't know enough about Calvinism to critique it, because that is what the Calvinist appears to be saying. However, the Calvinist's meaning is hidden. What he is really saying is the interlocutor doesn't know "his unique" understanding of Calvinism. Which, of course would be obvious, and therefore easy to prove, because every Calvinist is his own unique snowflake, having his own unique understanding of Calvinism, where he resides somewhere on the continuum line of determinism, in a location where he feels comfortable living with its dark implications.

He might be an ultra-soft-determinist.

He might be a moderate-determinist.

He might be a semi-hard-determinist.

He might be a hard-determinist.

The Calvinist is quite correct; the interlocutor can't possibly know his particular and unique understanding of Calvinism. In the event, the interlocutor doesn't recognize the subtle play in wording, he will lunge head-on, full speed into a bright red cape.

In order to meet this challenge, if it is indeed asserted in earnest, the interlocutor must have done his due diligence well in advance. He must have a full and comprehensive factual knowledge of quotes from leading Calvinists, and he must be able to enunciate them, unemotionally, accurately, in a sequence that is non-aggressive, intelligent, rational, and lucid. The Calvinist knows, if the interlocutor doesn't have the ability to do all that, he can be dismissed out of hand.

The interlocutor must also be prepared for the Calvinist to deviate from the leading enunciations of Calvinism and represent his own unique understanding of

Calvinism. The interlocutor must be keenly prepared for this strategy, and know how to quickly respond. If the Calvinist chooses that recourse, the dialog is then doomed, fruitless and destructive, as the interlocutor is at that point chasing after multiple rabbits, each having their own hole to escape into.

When that is the case it is best to disengage cordially, friendly, in a Christ-like manner. If any Christ-like, truth-seeking dialog is to be exchanged, it must be agreed, that the Calvinist will represent "core" Calvinism and not some unique illusive understanding of it.

Now assuming the interlocutor recognizes the bullfighter trick, and assuming he is able to respond accordingly, wisely and coherently, it is then the Calvinist's decision to continue the dialog or retreat. A retreat can come in a number of forms. The Calvinist can insist he doesn't have time for such dialog and leave. Or he can start throwing up red herrings to create a smokescreen, with the hopes that he can pull the interlocutor off balance. This tactic can be likened to putting a carrot in front of a mule, baiting the interlocutor with multiple carrots, leading him forward with each one, in order to trip him up.

The baiting carrot technique is a strategy which allows the Calvinist to retain control over both parties' dialog, leading the interlocutor around in circles, and baiting him, with the hopes he will trip over himself, which is most likely the case. If the interlocutor can recognize the carrot technique, and he is able to reestablish control over his part of the dialog, it can continue, with the hopes it portends the pursuit of truth. The interlocutor should be keenly on the lookout for clues within the Calvinist's dialog, to ascertain whether there is a focus on the pursuit of truth or a focus on winning. When the latter is the case, again, the interlocutor should immediately disengage cordially. When one partner is focused on winning, whether it be the Calvinist or the interlocutor, both parties lose.

The person who appears to have lost walks away confused, and the person who wins walks away satisfied, but actually becomes the bigger loser, because his winning has simply reinforced his own self-deceptions.

Another technique is for the Calvinist to pull additional Calvinists into the dialog with the hopes of drawing the interlocutor into a game of tag, which will almost always result in the interlocutor's slaughter. At that point the interlocutor will be faced fending off multiple aggressors. This type of event, unfortunately resembles a wolf-pack going after prey. It's best to be wary of it and cautious about getting lured into it.

The interlocutor is not doing himself or the Calvinist any favors by pursuing this course, as it quickly devolves into a dog-eat-dog event, which is destructive for Christians to engage in. Again, this technique is an indicator that the focus is not on a pursuit of truth, but on winning. It's easy to get psychologically invested in the dialog, and postpone disengagement. But one must be keenly on the lookout for "winning" or "competition" indicators. When a sincere and earnest and open-minded pursuit of truth is not at work (and in most cases it won't be), the continuation of dialog is doomed to be fruitless and destructive. It's best to be Christ-like and be about your father's business.

Part 33. Listing a few Calvinist types for those who are unprepared:

Many mainstream Christians, without an understanding of the least visible and foundational component of Calvinism, are simply unprepared for truth-seeking, non-aggressive dialog with them. The following list will help the reader understand what he might be facing, and offer a few words of advice in advance.

Ultra-soft determinist Calvinists are most often the Calvinists, who, by virtue of the fact they are members of a reformed church, are most likely to locate themselves as close as possible to the extreme indeterminist end of the line of determinism. Thinking about the darker implications of sovereignty is uncomfortable for them. And so they simply refuse to think about it. This Calvinist will usually respond in shock and bewilderment to criticisms of Calvinism, since his perception of Calvin and Calvinism is only benevolent, by virtue of the fact he prevents himself from recognizing its dark implications. Initiating critical-thinking dialog with this Calvinist is mostly likely fruitless. His mind is full of doublespeak mantras he has been taught, which the system engineers to minimize cognitive dissonance and retain belief. He's not a critical thinker. He's not emotionally prepared to face a rational examination of the system. He has mostly good feelings towards the Calvinist assembly he attends, and so He's happy right where he is. Unless his love for Jesus can draw him into a pursuit of truth, he will remain there, as a dedicated, happy disciple, probably for life. Remaining cordial and friendly and avoiding dialog in Calvinist controversies should foster your most fruit-full interactions with this believer.

The **moderate determinist** is the more serious Calvinist. He is a critical thinker. He can be likened to Plato's Spartan warrior. He has a bent towards philosophy and intellectualism. He learns Aristotelian logic and how to recognize fallacious arguments. He puts more focus on memorizing Calvin's arguments of defense. He reads current leading Calvinists and memorizes their promotion techniques and defense arguments. He has an urgency to propagate the system. He understands and accepts his need to rationalize dishonesty, by deploying the standard semantic games used by the current star enunciators. He may have aspirations to be a star warrior himself one day, honored and revered by his peers. He may be sharpening his Aristotelian sword, hoping for a chance to slice the opponent, and experience the endorphin rush. His pastor or other skilled Calvinists may be mentoring him for future semantic duals. He is learning the Calvinist's skill and trade. He's getting himself ready to slice up the enemy on the battlefield of language.

The next Calvinist on the line of determinism is quite possibly **the pastor**. He has gone well beyond the Spartan warrior phase. He is dedicated to the recruitment, retention, and maintenance of the Calvinist fold, and the work expected of him to maximize Calvinism's domination over its competitors. He has learned how to wear the mask of "Speaking with authority, not as the Scribes and Pharisees". He knows how to walk softly and carry a big stick. He wants to be a skilled Esau, who can please his Calvinist fathers and bring home the bacon. He may have the utmost adoration of the churches starry-eyed Spartan warriors, who follow him around like a flock of little ducklings. He writes stern commentaries on serious church subjects, which he knows will never see any form of scholarly peer review, and which most of his flock will embrace—and as the proverb says: "believe every word". He knows how to scrunch his eyebrows and modulate his "Moses" voice. His congregation has no idea of the degree to which their relationship to him is based on dependency. He gains access to the personal lives of his flock, and thus has the ability to hold his knowledge of their indiscretions over their heads—in a pastoral loving way of course.

If he doesn't have a flock of his own, he has no problems cutting a baby (i.e., an existing congregation) in half, in order to get Calvin's share. He may be applying for pastor-ship of some unsuspecting non-Calvinist congregation, for the purpose of surreptitiously accomplishing a violent takeover of the church and its properties. He will do this by lying about his Calvinistic ties and intentions. He knows how to implement thought reform. Once in the church he will immediately start implementing standard Calvinist radicalization policies, sending away for free Calvinist indoctrination materials and implementing bible studies. He is on the lookout for anyone in the congregation who may catch-on to his strategy, and if so, he will do whatever it takes to get rid of them. His is a holy war, and he its committed Jihadist, who has no problem with the sacred-lie. Once the congregation has been Calvinized, and the sign outside says "reformed", and the property legally secured, he can relax, wear the mask of the good shepherd, keep the congregation under his psychological control, walk in the pastoral glow, and enjoy the fruits of his labors.

The next Calvinist up the power hierarchy is most likely a **star player** on the current Calvinist stage. He probably has multiple PhDs, and may be a very successful pastor or theologian-philosopher. He is one of the authors of a continuous stream of Calvinist books, which are never-ever-ever-ever-ever advertised as Calvinist. He is at the top of the Calvinist skill-set in semantic magicianry. His ability at spinning doublespeak is simply hypnotizing, and everything he writes and says is a proliferation of semantic tricks and word games. He may have scheduled appearances on Christian radio or television. He is at the top of his game. He is one of the commanding officers in the Calvinist army, who has a cult-like following. He is a Napoleon on the battlefield. He is a goliath with a Cheshire-cat smile, who broadcasts out powerful challenges to anyone challenge-able. If he challenges you, you had better be a David, and have five smooth stones and a sling, or he'll feed your flesh to the birds and wild animals.

The next Calvinist on the continuum line of determinism is the **illusive Hard Determinist**. For him, free will in any form is a total illusion. He asserts God as the author of every conceivable hideous sin and evil, without blushing or blinking. It makes perfect sense to him. While he perceives himself as the true Calvinist, he is what other Calvinist's call Hyper. He is often a phantom to outsiders and keeps himself out of public discourse for the sake of Calvinism's reputation, (unless he's a member of the Wesboro group). If you ever meet this illusive creature, it will be a once in a lifetime event and you might want to get his autograph.

The next Calvinist is the one we all love. He is the **quintessential scholar**. He is peer reviewed and may be honored as one of the leaders in biblical scholarship. He never lets his Calvinism compromise his integrity. His commentaries are highly informative and wonderfully balanced. He has no urgency to persuade his appreciative readers into Calvinism. He simply does what the best scholars do best…he lays out the facts, and the arguments from all sides, and leaves you free to draw your own conclusions. He is not afraid of speaking the truth in love, when he recognizes things he doesn't find Christ-like in the Calvinist fold. He is the Calvinist every sincere Christian lover of truth and lover of Jesus, love's to love. We are extremely fortunate that God blessed him with all of his faculties and high ethics. You're every encounter with this Calvinist will be a Godly blessing. He will hear God say "well done good and faithful servant".

He is the exception and not the rule.

Part 34. Calvinism's primary urgencies are observed as Christianized dishonesty:

We have previously described the story of a young man who relies upon misleading language in order to forward his goals with a young woman at lover's lane. We've described the reasons why Calvinists are driven to use misleading language tactics. This section will be dedicated to detailing ways in which dishonest language has become the norm for Calvinists.

People who are exposed to Calvinistic preaching often relate a feeling of discomfort and puzzlement they sense, as they do not understand its religio-philosophical foundation as Universal Divine Causal Determinism. Calvinists themselves, have a considerable urgency to promote their doctrines because they have been convinced they have the "true" gospel and all other Christians are deluded. Calvinists therefore work very hard at painting their doctrines with a brush of benevolence in order to give the product the greatest degree of marketability. We can see that there are some very stark aspects to Calvin's view of God and His disposition towards mankind. We understand that false advertising is the strategy of obfuscating the products unappealing aspects, while inflating lauded aspects in order to induce buy-in. When one starts to examine Calvinist language carefully, one will observe the same urgencies and semantic devices consistently at work.

An article posted at the web-site; Do-Right-Christians, titled Calvinist dishonesty states: "When witnessing to Mormons, Jehovah's Witnesses, Catholics, etc… one thing you will discover quickly is that each appear to be religious and sometimes even using orthodox or theologically correct sounding language. For example, a

Jehovah's Witness will claim to believe that Jesus is the Son of God. However, that's not all there is to the story. Once you learn to get beyond the language barrier, you learn that you are not speaking the same language as they are.

Calvinism has the same problem. If Calvinists are going to demand that they be treated as and respected as Bible believing Christians, then they need to start being accountable for their consistently dishonest representations of the gospel, and be straight up with people about what they truly believe and about what they really mean when they use commonly familiar theological terms. Some Calvinists do not even notice themselves doing this, which is what leads to the oft-used popular Calvinist mantra "You don't understand Calvinism". With the standards that Calvinists demand for "understanding Calvinism", nobody should be expected to "understand" it and have any meaningful debate on the matter so long as the Calvinist refuses to face his dishonest representations of what he truly believes. The very fact that the Calvinists employ such rhetoric to maintain credibility among religious factions is in itself cause for concern. We are naturally skeptical of a salesman that we think is hiding something about the product he's trying to sell, and we hope that people use the same critical thinking with their Biblical knowledge and common sense when it comes to evaluating Calvinism."

John MacArthur (1939), a leading pastor and promoter of Calvinism, calls his ministry "Grace to you", which is obviously a benevolent sounding name. But just like our young man at lover's lane, what is being obfuscated is the "type" of "Grace", he has in mind.For mainline Christianity, "Grace" is defined as God's unmerited favor and benevolence towards mankind, especially seen in the sacrifice of Jesus for the salvation of fallen sinful man. However, within the Calvinist system of glorified-evil dualism, "Grace", like most other things, has a light-side, and a dark-side, and is commonly defined as God specifically designing the vast majority of the human population for eternal torments, for His good pleasure.

Calvinism's definition of "Grace" is therefore radically different, containing both a light-side and a dark-side. Using "Grace" terminology in a dishonest manner to the unsuspecting, represents a potent tool for promoting the product. Mr. MacArthur will appear on mainstream Christian radio and TV programming, enunciating "Grace", using the same exact strategy of our young man at lover's lane. The Calvinists urgency to promote the product, coupled with the general distaste within mainstream Christianity for glorified-evil, drives them to the consistent use of dishonest marketing strategies.

The euphemistic terms "Doctrines of Grace" and "Irresistible Grace" are also terms that seek to paint the product as benevolent while camouflaging the dark-side of its grace. The underlying model, hidden behind benevolent terms is that God takes special pleasure in designing humans for an eternal lake of fire in order to manifest His glory.

Calvinists are intensely involved in marketing the product through published books, radio broadcasts, and TV programming. And in the vast majority of these forms of media, they are extremely careful to conceal Calvinism, because they know: the book would be given away—the radio turned off—the TV switched to another channel. And so they consistently promote the system using various cloaking techniques.

Recently a Christian woman related the first time she heard a specific minister on Christian Television. At first she was puzzled by his words and demeanor. Obviously, there were absolutely not indicators it was Calvinism. When asked to be more descriptive, she used the words "harsh", "stoic", "condescending", and "non-empathetic". On a later occasion she confirmed the man she saw was named John MacArthur. She didn't know what label to put on what she was hearing and seeing, but she did know how to describe it.

Stoicism, (a resolution to divine fate), is an honored component Calvinists are very proud of. The Greek stoics likewise honored their resolution, because resting in fate allowed them to submit their lives to the divine providence of the gods.

Calvinist Paul Helm, a Teaching Fellow in Philosophical Theology, in an article titled Calvin and the Stoics writes: "It is clear that Calvin, though ostensibly taking a via media between fortune and chance on the one hand, and Stoic necessity/fatalism on the other is, like his mentor Augustine, in virtue of his commitment to divine sovereignty, inclined more to the side of fatalism than to the side of fortune and chance, or to some view of providence which has to find place for the 'contingency which depends on human will'. The sense of fortuitousness is purely epistemic, since necessity is the basic metaphysical component in his account of providence."

Derk Pereboom, Professor of Philosophy, Cornell University in Theological Determinism and Divine Providence writes: "In the Stoic view, God determines everything that happens in accord with the good of the whole universe, while the nature of this good is incompletely understood on our part."

See if you can guess the author of the following quote: "For if god had so arranged his own part, which he has given to us as a fragment of himself, that it would be hindered or constrained by himself or by anyone else, he would no longer be god. Nor would he be caring for us as he ought."

Is the above quote from John Calvin or Epictetus?

Calvinist, John Piper, in his book Does God Desire Everyone to be Saved attempts to define the Calvinist vs. the non-Calvinist position where he writes: "Both (Calvinists and non-Calvinists) can say that God wills for all to be saved. And when queried why all are not saved, both Reformed and Arminians answer the same: because God is committed to something more valuable than saving all."

Here Mr. Piper's language works to make two misrepresentations.

Firstly, it works to misrepresent Calvinism's reading of the text, by implying that the Calvinist reads the "plain reading" of the text, while the language also obfuscates the fact that the Calvinist's reading adds implicit distinctions into the text which are not explicitly there. Secondly his language works to misrepresent the non-Calvinist interpretation of the same text.

In his first misrepresentation, his language hides the fact that Calvin clearly, and forcibly asserts that God does NOT will for all men to be saved, else they would be.

If Mr. Piper stated this unambiguously, it would raise the specter that Calvin's assertion appears to contradict the text. If one reads the text without inserting additional implicit distinctions into it, the verse asserts simply that God DOES desire for all men to be saved. And on this view, Calvin's forcible assertion would then appear to be a direct contradiction. So then, in order to have the text interpreted so as to assert that God does NOT will all men to be saved, without physically altering the text, additional implicit distinctions must be added into the text at the time of reading.

It should be obvious how radically contradictory the resulting two interpretations become. One interpretation asserts that God DOES will all men to be saved, while the other asserts God does NOT.

Here it might be instructive to detail the Square of Opposition; a basic law of logic, which states that there are four possible types of propositions:

 1. Universal Positive proposition.

 2. Universal Negative proposition.

 3. Particular Positive proposition.

 4. Particular Negative proposition.

Examples:

 1. "ALL" humans "ARE" mammals.

 2. "NO" humans "ARE" mammals.

 3. "SOME" humans "ARE" mammals.

 4. "SOME" humans "ARE NOT" mammals.

In the Square of Opposition, propositions 1 and 4 directly contradict each other, and cannot both be true at the same time—one must be false. Also, both particular propositions (3 & 4) are corollaries of each other, where one follows from the other.

If one reads the scripture without added implicit distinctions, it asserts a Universal Positive proposition. God desires "ALL" men saved. However, to affirm the doctrine of Universal Divine Causal Determinism, Calvin must clearly reject the universal proposition that God wills all men saved. Calvin asserts that God wills "SOME" men saved (Proposition 3), and its corollary; God wills "SOME" men "NOT" saved (Proposition 4). If the text is to be read with Calvin's added implicit distinctions, it logically entails both the Particular Positive, and its corollary, Particular Negative, propositions. This is why some Calvinists use the term "Particular" redemption.

Mr. Piper is using language, which is strategically ambiguous enough to mislead the reader into believing he is asserting that Calvinism reads the text without implicit distinctions added into it, which is a clear obfuscation of the truth. We take note of Mr. Piper's very strategic choice of words: "Both 'CAN SAY' that God wills for all to be saved." This is a clear obfuscation of the whole truth, by the techniques of semantic under-specification and equivocating on the term "CAN SAY". Here Mr. Piper is simply not telling the truth, the whole truth, and nothing but the truth.

Yes, the Calvinist "CAN SAY" that God wills all men saved. But the truth is, the Calvinist "CAN SAY" it while meaning the opposite. And that strategy of language is in fact an example of Christianized dishonesty. Just like our young man at lover's lane, the Calvinist knows that if he speaks clearly, and honestly, without using subtle language techniques, he cannot simply say that God wills all men saved.

Mr. Piper will then assert his second misrepresentation of the non-Calvinist's handling of the text, by implying it is inferior because the non-Calvinist values "self-determination" more than he values God's sovereignty. But this argument also misses the mark. Firstly, the non-Calvinist is not forced into the unfortunate position of having to add implicit distinctions into the text, which are not explicitly there. Secondly, the primary difference between the theologies is the philosophical distinction of determinism. The non-Calvinist does not hold to Universal Divine Causal Determinism as the model of the universe, nor as a lens through which one reads scripture—while the Calvinist does.

However, it remains to be seen whether holding to causal determinism or not makes one position superior to the other, for the simple reason that what makes a theology superior or inferior, is in fact, its truth-value. The Calvinist can declare his theology (the superior one, which honors God the most) all he wants too. But if Universal Divine Causal Determinism is false, then how can a theology based upon it honor God? Is God honored by falsehoods? However, if Universal Divine Causal Determinism is true, then the Calvinist's assertion that his theology honors God can certainly be acknowledged.

However, if someday man discovers that Universal Divine Causal Determinism is false, then that which gives Calvinism it's most honored and adored distinctive, and which sets it apart from other theologies, has become Calvin's appalling disgrace. In that event, one can only surmise how Calvin would be desperate for God's benevolence, rather than for His glorified-evil, utilitarian sovereignty.

Mr. Piper continues his misleading language by stating: "The answer that Arminians give is that human self-determination and the possible loving relationship with God are more valuable than saving ALL people by sovereign, efficacious grace". By now, you should be able to see where Mr. Piper's language continues to be dishonest, where he says: "more valuable than saving 'ALL' people by sovereign, efficacious grace".

Mr. Piper is now equivocating on the word "ALL". The language is designed to give the appearance that Calvinism asserts God desires "ALL" to be saved "universally", while obfuscating the fact that in this verse Calvinist exegesis redefines the word "ALL" as meaning "SOME". The word ALL is mentally changed to the word SOME while reading the text. Again, the Calvinist is careful not to physically alter the text. So, he is taught to mentally insert the definition for the word SOME, when he reads the word ALL within the text. By doing so, the text becomes a Particular Positive proposition, along with its Particular Negative corollary. But the dishonesty becomes evident, when he represents the text "As If" it is a Universal Positive Proposition, while secretly holding to the opposite.

What is found to be most troubling about Calvinism then, is not the fact that it is based upon a particular doctrine of philosophy, but rather the consistent use of semantic trickery, which one must acknowledge has become its primary strength. Remembering Jerry Wall's reflection of this: "If Calvinists didn't rely upon misleading rhetoric, Calvinism would lose all credibility within two years".

Psalm 115:4-8, speaks in general terms, of man's crafting of false Gods. But it also reveals a critical principle when it states: "They that worship them become like them." Simply put; the character that we attribute to the deity we worship, will eventually become our character. When we hold to deity who chooses to mislead his people when he speaks, we will become like him. We become whom we worship.

Part 35. Lawyer-speak—how to avoid calling a spade a spade:

H. P. Grice (1988), a British philosopher of language, applied a primary focus on the nature of meaning and its implications within the philosophical study of semantics. He is known for coining the term: "implicature" within the "pragmatic" sub-field of linguistics. Grice, defines the implicature as a language technique which powerfully promotes meaning by "suggestion", couched in terminology which facilitates plausible deniability.

Noam Chomsky (1928) an American linguist, philosopher, and cognitive scientist, is often described as "the father of modern linguistics". In his work Requiem of the American Dream, Chomsky analyzes the language of presidential candidates and notes an extreme expertise in the use of implicatures, where language is used to powerfully "suggest" campaign promises ingeniously crafted as linguistic illusions. Chomsky notes: "The point is to create uninformed consumers who will make irrational choices. That's what advertising is all about. And when the same PR system runs elections, they do it the same way. They want to create an uninformed electorate, which will make irrational choices, often against their own interests. And we see it every time one of these extravaganzas takes place.

Right after the last election, the president won an award from the advertising industry, for the best marketing campaign in American history. The international business press executives were euphoric. They said we've been marketing candidates like toothpaste….and this is the greatest achievement we have. Firstly, the president didn't really promise anything. That's mostly illusion. You go back to the campaign rhetoric and take a look at it."

In the 1980s, Wanda Brandstetter, a volunteer working for ratification of the Equal Rights Amendment, handed her business card to a member of the Illinois House of Representatives, and on the back wrote: "Mr. Swanstrom the offer to help in your election and $1,000 for your campaign for Pro ERA vote". She was charged under the Illinois bribery statute with offering "personal advantage and property" to Representative Swanstrom.

The appellate judges looking at the case reflected that her language in the note "differed only subtly" from normal language commonly used within the gray areas of political finance, and which are often highly reliant upon implicatures and plausible deniability, in order to technically remain within the boundaries of the law. However, her conviction was upheld.

Lawyers are required to become experts in the use of language. One type of Lawyer-speak then, is the crafting of sentences, in such a way as to project a meaning the recipient is guaranteed to acquire, while also selecting words with a high precision of ambiguity, sufficient to ensure the author cannot be held legally or ethically accountable to the message. This type of language is used to draw the recipient into an agreement, which he would otherwise avoid, if the language were precise and unambiguous.

The language of marketing makes much use of the strategy of asserting highly explicit premises, followed by ambiguous conclusions, or no conclusion at all. This strategy works to lead the consumer into assuming the conclusion, without the advertising language having to clearly state it. Thus the consumer assumes all liability.

This technique can be readily used in asserting premises, which are highly "suggestive" of man as robotic, while leaving the conclusion of the argument ambiguous or unstated. Thus leading the recipient to perceive man as a robot without technically stating it. This tactic can be used to draw an unsuspecting recipient into the system's doublethink. If however, the recipient recognizes the doublethink, the Calvinist can then side step by accusing the recipient of misrepresenting the system.

When the Calvinist asserts, you don't understand Calvinism, what he is often observing is that you don't embrace the doublethink. The way the Calvinist often recognizes when one doesn't embrace Calvinism is by observing the absence of its doublespeak.

Take for example, Calvinism's highly marketed phrases "Irresistible Grace", and "Unconditional Election". These euphemisms are designed to draw the recipient into perceiving Calvinism as a doctrine of divine-benevolence, by emphasizing the light; "yin" side of the system, while the divine-malevolence element, contained within the dark; "yang" side of the system is obfuscated. The underlying foundational presupposition that God conceives, determinatively causes, and meticulously renders certain all that comes to pass is being obfuscated by these terms.

The potter and clay conception which asserts that God designs "vessels of honor", for salvation, as well as "vessels of wrath", for damnation, for his good pleasure, is being obfuscated. These terms are designed to hide the dark-side of the system. Such phrases work wonderfully also to retain the ranks of Soft Determinist Calvinists who refuse to acknowledge the dark-side. These persons can then be deployed as an army of unwitting recruiters, who will advertise the doctrine using highly engineered half-truths to unsuspecting recipients.

When one understands that in a world in which every event is causally determined and meticulously rendered certain, millennia before those events occur, then one understands that in such a world, absolutely everything man does is irresistible and unconditional.

And so, the light; "yin" side of the system contains "irresistible grace" and "unconditional election", while the dark; "yang" side contains "irresistible damnation", and "unconditional reprobation". But the Soft Determinist can conveniently refuse to acknowledge the dark-side of the system, so that he is guaranteed to only see and advertise its light-side.

Since Calvinism evolved from the synchronization of dualistic, "yin-yang", concepts, the system inherently contains a dualistic view of God and cosmos, in which good and evil are both equally necessary, which results in a doctrine of "necessary-evil". But how to get the bible reader to embrace that doctrine is tricky business, as he is instructed to abhor evil.

For example, Proverbs 16:17 says: "The way of the upright is to depart from evil, and he who keeps God's way preserves his soul." Verses like this give a clear inference that man is to abhor evil, because God Himself abhors evil. Therefore, the mainstream bible reader rejects the idea that God would take pleasure in the perpetration of evil.

However, the scripture also gives occasional and clear indicators that God does initiate evil. For example, that God sent an evil spirit to King Saul. Exodus 32 14 states that God repented of the evil which He thought to do to his people. So the mainstream bible reader does acknowledge that God occasionally initiates evil. But this understanding can then be co-opted by first persuading the recipient to embrace the assertion that everything God does, He does "for his good pleasure". Once that concept is accepted, it can be coupled with the biblical knowledge that God initiates evil. This then can be used to affirm a "yin-yang", glorified-evil, dualistic worldview, which entails God taking pleasure in initiating evil, and evil as necessary for the manifestation of His glory.

However, the Calvinist is keenly aware, even with this line of reasoning, his assertions may be rejected on ethical grounds. So to compensate for the arguments weakness, he adds persuasive, misleading language in order to draw the recipient into accepting an argument, which they would otherwise reject, if enunciated unambiguously.

Let's say for example, a Calvinist uses implicatures to suggests actions on God's part, that would commonly be defined by the adjective: "sadistic". The recipient then may emotionally respond by complaining that the Calvinist has painted God as a "sadist". The Calvinist can then respond by saying:

> "Did I say the word sadist? I didn't use the word sadist!
>
> Did you hear me say sadist?
>
> You obviously don't understand Calvinism!
>
> We would never call God a sadist!"

God is righteous in all His ways! The technique here is to assert a concept while rejecting its common label. This type of linguistic strategy also appears in Calvinist enunciations of their view of human free will, where they describe man using implicatures to suggest actions on man's part that would commonly be understood by the noun: "robot".

If the Calvinist is questioned on this, he might simply respond by saying:

> "Did I say the word robot?
> I didn't use the word robot!
> Did you hear me say robot?
> You obviously don't understand Calvinism!
> We would never call man a robot!"

Or, it would be common for a recipient to accuse the Calvinist with: "Calvinism teaches that God predestines man to hell". To this the Calvinist can respond: "We don't **say** it that way!". These semantic techniques work to allow the enunciator to construct descriptions that would commonly infer evil, and then ascribe a benevolent noun, verb, adverb, or adjective, to that description. Such techniques then work, to blur the lines of distinction between the positive-negative, light-dark, good-evil sides of the system. Calvinistic phrases are remarkably ingenious.

He doesn't have to call a spade a spade, because it's so easy for him to rely upon precisely crafted ambiguous language, designed to make spades appear as hearts. He learns lawyer-speak from the master lawyer and architect of the system.

Part 36. Drawing the unsuspecting into the pack with the dog-whistle:

According to William Safire (1929), author on language, the term "dog whistle" refers to the strategic crafting of words within surveys, to manipulate its outcome or manipulate opinion. Richard Morin, senior editor of the Pew Research Center states: "Dog-Whistle language is use of subtle changes in words, which guarantee remarkably different responses from unsuspecting recipients."
Political researchers take advantage of this, calling it the 'Dog Whistle Effect'. That is to say, you frame words to get the dog to move in your direction. In the marketing of products, Dog-Whistle language is used to make the product appealing to the greatest number of possible recipients, while alienating the smallest possible number. The danger with dog-whistle language within Christian theological dialog is that it achieves buy-in by undermining linguistic honesty.

Part 37. A lawyer tempts Jesus—Jesus' two-phased test, and how He reclaims a word's definition:

Behold, a certain lawyer stood up, and tempted Jesus saying; Master, what shall I do to inherit eternal life? And Jesus knew he was a lawyer, and that he was cunning in the handling of words. And Jesus knew the lawyer had devised a way to exegete God's love, so as to make it limited and conditional, and that the lawyer performed this exegesis, by manipulating the definition of one single word.

So Jesus tested the lawyer by asking him two separate and distinct questions:

(1) What does the text of scripture say?

(2) How do you exegete it? Now the lawyer suspected that Jesus might just know what he was up to.

So he attempted to obfuscate, by carefully answering only Jesus' first question. After all, he thought to himself, what harm can it do to simply quote scripture? So the lawyer quoted the text verbatim, and then remained silent, hoping Jesus wouldn't notice he avoided the second question. Now when Jesus heard him quote the text verbatim, including God's command to love one's "neighbor" as ones self, Jesus said; You have answered right. But Jesus was familiar with the lawyer's game, so he added; Follow the scripture as you have clearly stated it, and you shall live.

Now the lawyer understood that if he walked away in agreement at this point, he would not appear the winner. So his urgency impelled him. He smiled slightly at Jesus, and leaned forward confidently saying; But who is my neighbor?

Neighbor; was the one single word he was manipulating. You see, the lawyer was gambling that

Jesus wouldn't figure out his trick because very few had. But Jesus was more than familiar with exegetical word games. However, Jesus; reflecting God's love, hoped the lawyer would be open to God's love; which hopes all things.

So Jesus told him a parable—something like this:

A certain man, who was a Spanish theologian, physician, cartographer, and renaissance humanist, while traveling was attacked, stripped, beaten and left for dead. Then came a great lawyer theologian carrying his latest publication, who looked down at the man and said: "If my authority is worth anything, I will never permit him to depart alive" —and with that the lawyer theologian passed over.

Then came a second man, who was a highly popular pastor apologist philosopher who was a faithful standard bearer of the great lawyer theologian. And the second man looked down at him and said; this man is totally depraved, a vessel of wrath, which God has meticulously rendered certain, would use his free agency for his own damnation—and so he also passed over.

But then a certain semi-pelagian came, finding the man close to death. And he had compassion on the man, and bound up his wounds, and used his best oil and wine to bandage and refresh the man. And he set him on his horse while he himself walked, and brought him to an inn, and there took great care of him. And in the morning he departed giving money and instructions to the innkeeper for the man's hospitalization, saying take care of him; and I will pay all of his expenses.

Then Jesus turned to the lawyer who had so far evaded his second question, and asked him "which man best meets God's definition for the word "neighbor", the one who helped, or the one who passed over? Which man best exemplifies a "type" of love which hopes all things?

Now at this the Lawyer was speechless, realizing he could not escape Jesus' question. Jesus stood facing him, not flinching; not moving a muscle; patiently waiting. And suddenly, the lawyer's conscience, which had been dormant for so many years, now seemed to awaken. And he looked into Jesus' face, and saw the radiant love of Father God in His eyes. And before he knew what he was doing, he said; "The one who doesn't pass over is the one who best exemplifies a love that hopes all things".

Then Jesus smiled at the lawyer, gladly nodded, looked up to heaven, and honored the Holy Father, whose love can bring light into a man's heart. And Jesus said to him; Go my friend, and do not pass over anyone bleeding and dying on the road of life.

Part 38. Decoding obfuscations, euphemisms, equivocations and plausible deniability:

A euphemism isn't necessarily doublespeak. There are times when we use a euphemism to show our concern and care for another person's feelings, for example, at the death of a loved one. But this is not doublespeak, simply because the information exchanged between parties is based upon a common understanding which entails full disclosure. In other words, there is no intent for the author to mislead the recipient.

When the euphemism becomes doublespeak is when it is used to hide something. Typically because the author wants to achieve buy-in, which cannot occur without the recipient being mislead. And this use of euphemisms is then clearly a form of dishonesty.

There is a very distinct but often hidden difference between the "meaning " and the "sense" of a statement. The recipient must discover the "sense" of the message which may be cloaked, giving the statement multiple or ambiguous meanings.

The work of decoding a message so as to discover the "sense" and the "meaning", must take into account: the "intention", the "modalities", the "polyphony", the "communication scenario", and the "connotation", but most importantly, it must accurately discern what is strategically unsaid. All of which the average non-Calvinist is ill prepared to do, when we consider the sheer magnitude of hidden presuppositions and implicatures, imbedded within Calvinism's normal mode of communication.

Misleading, "coded" words hide as much as they reveal, and always require multiple readings in order for one to accurately decipher what is and what is not being stated. Discerning what is being withheld, rather than what appears to be stated, then, is often the more critical part of decoding Calvinist language.

J.I. Packer, a noted Calvinist, authored the book: The Love of God: Universal and Particular. Firstly, we recognize Packer's keen understanding of Universal vs. Particular within logic, so we know that he is philosophically savvy about how Universal and Particular apply within Calvinistic distinctions. Secondly, we know that mainstream Christianity holds God's love as universal (i.e., God loves each individual as He loves all persons).

But the Calvinist; when logically consistent with Calvin holds that God's love is not universal (i.e., God does not love each individual as He loves all persons). Consistent with Calvinistic language, Packer's book title joins Universal and Particular together, which begs the question: is he going to assert what he doesn't believe? By now you already probably know the answer.

Remember, the Square of Oppositions. Here is how the four propositions logically relate:

(1) A "Universal Positive" can be joined with a "Particular Positive" and remain logically coherent.

(2) A "Universal Negative" and a "Particular Negative" can be joined together and remain logically coherent.

(3) A "Universal Positive" is logically contrary to a "Universal Negative", the two are incoherent.

(4) A "Universal Positive" and a "Particular Negative" are logical contradictions, the two are incoherent.

(5) A "Universal Negative" and a "Particular Positive" are logical contradictions, the two are incoherent.

If Packer tries to insist that God's love is both: "Universal Positive": (God DOES love each person as He loves all persons), with a "Universal Negative" (God DOES NOT love each person as He loves all persons), then he is asserting two contrary propositions which are logically incoherent.

In other words, God would not do two contrary things; "Positive-A" and "Negative-A" at the same time, because those two would negate each other, showing God to be incoherent, which is absurd.

So let's do some Calvinist language decoding:

He writes: "Everyone in the Reformed mainstream will insist that Christ the Savior is freely offered—indeed, freely offers himself—to sinners in and through the gospel; and that since God gives all free agency (that is, voluntary decision-making power) we are indeed answerable to him for what we do, first, about universal general revelation, and then about the law and gospel when and as these are presented to us… But Calvinism at the same time affirms the total, perversity, depravity, and inability of fallen human beings, which results in them naturally and continually using their free agency to say no to God".

Jerry Walls in "Why I am not a Calvinist" attempts to decode Packer's language. He writes: "So how does Packer understand the God-given free agency he invokes? Does he mean "A" that God gives all sinners the ability to respond positively to the offer of the gospel, and therefore all are answerable to him? Does grace make it possible to respond positively, even for those who end up responding negatively? Or does he mean "NOT A" only that everyone willingly (voluntarily) chooses as they have been determined to choose?

The first sentence quoted above implies the former view of freedom, whereas the second sentence is more in line with the latter view. Packer does not precisely state the nature of human freedom and responsibility, so his meaning remains uncertain."

Remember William Lane Craig's assessment that Calvinists consistently fall short of enunciating the "Radical Distinction" that is entailed within the system. Here Packer's statement is ambiguous enough to be interpreted in two ways, which are contrary to each other.

Proposition "A": Man's ability to choose, DOES have a consequentially determinative effect within the salvation process.

Proposition "NOT A": Man's ability to choose, DOES NOT have a consequentially determinative effect within the salvation process.

These two propositions are logically contrary to each other, and as we can see, Packer gives the appearance of stating both, while being ambiguous enough to leave us uncertain.

What we see here can be likened to the blowing two different dog-whistles at the same time. Some dogs will come to the first whistle "A", and reject the second "NOT A", while other dogs will respond the other way around. Walls is clear minded enough to realize that Packer is making an uncertain sound. But why? Surely a man like Packer is obviously: educated enough, sophisticated enough, clear minded enough—to know precisely what Calvinism insists. Does man's free will have any consequentially determinative role in the salvation process, or not? Why can't Packer simply enunciate what Calvinism insists precisely, and unambiguously? Why the doublespeak?

Perhaps Packer is speaking in As-If mode; knowing that a percentage of readers will agree with "A" and reject "NOT A", while others will respond the other way around. So he asserts both "A" and "NOT A" within imprecise language.

The Calvinist wants to hold man responsible for his role in the salvation process; As-If man's choice had a consequentially determinative role in that process, "A". But he also will not allow for man's choice to have any consequentially determinative role in that process, "NOT A". And he's smart enough to know that to clearly state both, is to assert something logically incoherent or distasteful and therefore detrimental for recruitment. So he must obfuscate using precise-ambiguity, in order to appeal to both propositions, while retaining plausible deniability.

Part 39. When "holy", "love", and "good" become ambiguous, what is there to trust:

In Genesis, the writer describes the serpent as "the most subtle beast of the field". Prior to Eve's conversation with the serpent in the garden, man's perception of God is of a benevolent loving father, who desires only their good. But above all, He is a person whom they can fully trust. But isn't it, in fact, His holiness, His love, and His goodness, that are being trusted? It is the serpent, which first induces mankind to perceive of a God who tells them He wills "A" while secretly He wills "NOT A". It is the serpent that induces mankind to perceive of God as having characteristics they cannot trust. So as the scripture says: "By one man's disobedience, sin came into the world."

But it was a beguiler who taught man to question God's benevolence, leading man to question God's sincerity, creating a question of trust. Again, we should distinguish the difference between withholding information and purposefully misleading information.

Later, we will see the Son of God, become the second Adam, again in the garden. This time He will say "Not my will but your will be done". Does Jesus anywhere give us the impression that his perception of Father God, is of one who represents His will to Jesus, as "A" while secretly willing "NOT 'A'"? We would be hard put to find scriptural evidence of Jesus having a perception of a Father who strategically misleads his son. Wouldn't it be true to say, that the reason Jesus can say "Not my will but your will be done" is because, for Jesus, God the Father is the only one in whom He can fully and completely trust?

But what is it about the Father that Jesus trusts? Is it merely the existence of the Father and His sovereignty? Or is it the consistent, repeatable dependable character and nature of the Father that Jesus trusts?

Jesus tells His disciples that not even He knows the day and the hour, the Father has set, so the Father doesn't reveal everything to Jesus. Again, it's one thing to withhold information, and quite another to purposefully deceive or mislead. Even husbands and wives have little things they withhold from each other, yet retain a high degree of trust. But once a partner starts to mislead another, trust dissolves.

Jesus certainly knew that the religious leaders could not be trusted. But what was it about the religious leaders that couldn't be trusted? He knows the religious leaders exist, just as much as He knows the Father exists. So the trust factor can't be hinged upon knowing they exist. Wasn't it, in fact, the way the religious leaders communicated, that Jesus couldn't trust?

I have never heard a Calvinist insist that God purposefully misled Jesus, the way Calvin insists God misleads mankind; communicating a "revealed" will "A" to Jesus, only for Jesus to find out later, God's "secret" will for Him was "NOT A"? Or leading Jesus to believe He is God's son at one point in time, only for Jesus to find out God's secret will was to condemn him. The Calvinist might assert that God's relationship with Jesus is different, because Jesus and God are one. And therefore, God wouldn't mislead Jesus the way Calvin asserts He does mankind. And that indeed would confirm that Calvin holds to a double standard.

But that assertion also works to compromise scripture's teaching that Jesus took upon Himself human form in order to be tempted in all things like as we. How can that be fulfilled, if God doesn't mislead Jesus, but He does mislead man? Wouldn't that compromise the impact of Jesus saying "Father, not my will but your will be done"?

Perhaps it is the serpent in the first garden, who plants the idea into Calvin's mind, that God misleads people when He speaks? In order for one to trust something, there has to be repeatability, which resolves to dependability.

Again, in the marriage relationship, husbands and wives know their partners exist, but that is not what determines their trust for each other. Trust is reliant upon honesty.

Even within organized crime, men have to agree to communicate honestly to each other, in order to maintain the organizations stability. If a wife observes that her husband repeatedly tells her the truth, her faith in her husband's dependability is strengthened, and she perceives him as a person who honors his word. But if she observes he consistently speaks "A" while secretly he means "NOT A", her faith in her husband's dependability dissolves, and she concludes he is not a person who honors his word. This is what "Faith" means.

If something's dependability is questionable, you can't have any significant type of "Faith" in it. In other words, "Faith" hinges upon *A Posteriori* knowledge, which in Calvin's view of God, is not available to us. You can however, have "Faith" that God exists and that He is sovereign, but you can't have *A Posteriori* knowledge, of what that means.

I suppose one could have "Faith" in the un-repeatability of God's love. But its inscrutable to me how one would call that a superior faith, because it resolves to a God with characteristics that cannot be trusted.

Can you trust God's "Grace"? Again, how can you trust what you don't know? Can you trust His benevolence? But you have no way of knowing what His benevolence will look like for you. It could be your blessing—or your eternal damnation. It would seem that on Calvin's view of God, all he has to trust in, is that God exists and that God is sovereign.

Calvin's descriptions of God's disposition for you as an individual leaves you without any concrete knowledge of what God's disposition for you will be. The Calvinist can of course choose to make-believe the dilemma doesn't exist. But choosing to ignore the elephant in the room only makes the elephant magically disappear in the one's mind. Some Calvinists will eventually have to bump up against the elephant in the room no matter how much he chooses to deny it exists. Since whether God seeks the Calvinist's eternal salvation or his eternal torture, are, for all intents and purposes, unknown, it would seem, the only substantive concepts concerning God, the Calvinist has to trust, are God's existence and His sovereignty.

Once one removes all of the ad hoc rescues, grasping at straws, and peripheral irrelevant arguments which would seek to camouflage this concern, the Calvinist (and of course we mean the one who remains true to Calvin) is left to trust and have faith, only that God exists, and that He is sovereign. For all else is: maybe good—maybe evil. In Calvin's dualistic system of glorified-evil, no one knows what his "LOT" in life will be, until it's his time to know.

Part 40. Protecting his flock from the wolves of his own conclusions—we don't say it that way:

There is a parable of a young girl who volunteered to work overseas, during her college summer vacation. She became fast friends with a local girl her age, who took it upon herself to introduce her to every aspect of their culture. One day while relaxing in the sun, next to a beautiful lake, she spotted a family walking on the beach; the mother carrying a baby. She watched the mother slowly give the infant to the husband, who walked out into the water and squatted. As she watched, her guest became very upset with her, insisting that she should mind her own business. It was then, she realized, she was witnessing the disposal of a female infant who had been born without official sanction. The reality of what she had just witnessed crept on her and fiercely gripped her throat, and she felt sick to her stomach.

"You shouldn't have watched" her guest told her sternly.

As they walked back to her apartment, she couldn't get the picture out of her mind.

"Are you ok?" her guest asked, before dropping her off.

She nodded her head to signify yes.

"We are not murderers, if that is what you are thinking!" her friend insisted glaring at her in anger.

"We are good people", she insisted.

"I sat there and watched a baby being murdered" covering her face, she blurted it out before she could stop herself.

"In our village, we don't say it that way", her guest replied.

"I don't understand…what do you mean?" she asked.

"What we say is: we gave the baby a bath, but the baby didn't survive".

Our parable shows us that different cultures have different forms of ethics, and instances in which ethical concerns differ significantly based upon life's pressures. In these instances, we can understand how people in such a culture would be concerned about how they are perceived by outsiders. And their use of language reflects those concerns. "We don't say it that way", is a linguistic tool we might readily find, reappearing, within many controversies over cultural, or ethical differences, especially when a difference may incite insult, disparagement, or other possible ramifications.

Calvinists; who exist within their own unique sub-culture, are real people, frequently facing real controversies, and ethical questions concerning their image of God. Being accused of honoring a God who commits hideous evils is not an unusual hardship for the Calvinist to face. And Calvinists, responding to their urgencies for expansion and recruitment are keenly aware of the demands encumbered upon them for maintaining the system's image as benevolent as possible.

And as has been said, those urgencies are reflected in their language. It would not be unusual to hear a

Calvinist retort: "We don't say it that way!" The dedicated Calvinist has a sincere urgency to keep the dark-side of the doctrine obscured from public view. For the Calvinist, language is the only real tool he has to propagate his doctrine, fend off disparagements, and keep the image clean and polished, with the hopes of maximizing recruitment. Calvinists are keenly aware that the key to whether their population expands or not, is "how they say it". Lawyer speak in religious garb is language highly reliant upon subtle technicalities, which facilitate plausible deniability.

You will notice that any predominate voice of Calvinism will hardly ever say God "designs" persons as vessels of wrath. Speaking that unambiguously would give away the power of implicatures. If you want to have a little fun with a Calvinist, ask him if God "makes" all things come to pass, and see if he doesn't respond with: "we don't say it that way".

Part 41. Final thanks—compassion and words of caution:

This then becomes the Calvinist's normalcy. They are highly reliant upon dishonest language without allowing themselves to recognize it as such. Once we understand the burdens the system imposes on them, and the socialization mechanisms, which re-form their thinking, we can see that they are under the similar burden of an individual forced to craft phrases for false advertisements, or speeches for cunning politicians.

And we can understand the social structure, which works to recruit and retain them into the system. Armed with this understanding, we can have compassion on the Calvinist, understanding why he thinks, behaves, and communicates the way he does.

But you should also be keenly ready for an almost endless supply of secret distinctions, which his tradition automatically applies to almost every word within every sentence, misleading one into thinking he is saying "A", when he is really saying both "A" and "NOT A" at the same time. Sometimes it's hard to get our heads around how doublespeak works. We need to slow, down and think every sentence through, in order to realize its hidden distinctions.

In order to not be misled, one has to carefully parse every word, treating each sentence as if it were encrypted. An understanding that his tradition is framed within a good-evil dualism and Universal Divine Causal Determinism, are the key to decoding his equivocal language, and recognizing that doublespeak is his normalcy, is critical to your success. It is advisable to give oneself plenty of opportunity and time to examine Calvinist distinctives from a safe distance, where one is not vulnerable to being unwittingly drawn in by persuasive words.

Margaret Thaler Singer (1921), a clinical psychologist and expert on persuasion, warns: "Everyone is influenced and persuaded daily in various ways. But your vulnerability to influence varies. The ability to fend off persuaders is reduced when you are rushed, stressed, uncertain, lonely, indifferent, uninformed, distracted, or fatigued. And your vulnerability is also affected by the status and power of the persuader"

Steven Hassan, author of "Releasing the Bonds – Empowering people to think for themselves" warns us that people of all walks of life, and status, no matter how highly educated, are drawn in by those who have a high expertise in the use of language. Everyone is vulnerable!

In vain is the net spread in the sight of any bird— Proverbs 1:17.

It is hoped that this writing has shed useful light on Calvinist thinking, behavior, and language.

We thank you, *the reader*, for bearing with, and making these things a part of your thoughtful considerations.

Abba! — Father!

To God Himself we cannot give a holier name.

William Wordsworth

Indicators of Calvinism to watch out for:

- Any references to John Calvin or Augustine as standards of Christianity.

- Any references to "Reformed" theology.
- Strange unique names ascribed to a group such as "Primitive Christian"
- Obvious linguistic dishonesties, semantic ambiguities, or word games.
- A highly sophisticated manner of speech, which may accompany overt doctrinal confidence.
- A Group which manifests a high authority model in its leadership
- Members of a group who are unaware their relationship to their leader is dependency based
- A Group or person who manifests above average doctrinal dogmatism or doctrinal obsession
- A Group or person who manifests above average doctrinal confidence
- The consistent honoring of historical persons, of a doctrinal tradition Exhibitions of religious pride or borderline elitism
- A demeanor of stoicism which leans towards theistic fatalism

Here is a related extract from a posting on the web from Bruce McLaughlin at Christian Apologetic.org: "If Calvinism is making uninvited, ninja-like infiltrations into your church or denomination and you decide to stand against it, be prepared for certain tactics frequently utilized by those who believe Calvinism should, for the greater good, dominate or at least co-exist.

Once the core conflicts of Calvinism/Arminianism can no longer be suppressed by clever strategies, the proponents of Calvinism will generally maneuver from a tactical playbook that includes some of the following items:

- Avoid admitting you are a Calvinist.
- Avoid engaging your opponents with logic and reason.
- Erect a few "straw-man" arguments, attribute them to your opponents and then show their weaknesses. (A typical straw-man argument erected by Calvinists is that Arminians believe in salvation by works because the act of free will acceptance is a "work." But Scripture never portrays a choice to receive a gift from God as a "work.")
- Never advocate the full face of Calvinism; instead, gradually weave theological threads into the preaching and teaching of the church.
- Assert that Calvinist men and women are hard working persons of the highest integrity whose motives are beyond reproach.
- Suggest that your opponents are divisive, narrow minded, mean spirited and instruments of discord.
- Assert the intellectual, academic and spiritual superiority of Calvinist theologians and spokespersons.

- Extol the magnificence of the Reformation and the Reformers.
- Teach that peace and unity are more important than some antiquated concept of truth."

www.ingramcontent.com/pod-product-compliance
Lightning Source LLC
Chambersburg PA
CBHW051604250726